AGRICULTURAL SCIENCE
for the
CARIBBEAN

Ralph Persad

T0347005

OXFORD
UNIVERSITY PRESS

OXFORD
UNIVERSITY PRESS

Great Clarendon Street, Oxford, OX2 6DP, United Kingdom

Oxford University Press is a department of the University of Oxford.
It furthers the University's objective of excellence in research, scholarship,
and education by publishing worldwide. Oxford is a registered trade mark of
Oxford University Press in the UK and in certain other countries

Text © Nelson Thornes Ltd 1977, 1994, 2003

First published by Thomas Nelson and Sons Ltd in 1977
Second edition published by Thomas Nelson and Sons Ltd in 1994
Third edition published by Nelson Thornes Ltd in 2003
This edition published by Oxford University Press in 2014

British Library Cataloguing in Publication Data
Data available

978-0-1756-6395-8

25

Printed and bound by CPI Group (UK) Ltd, Croydon, CR0 4YY

Acknowledgements

Illustrations: Ray Burrows, Corinne Clark and Ricardo Moratalla

The author and publisher wish to thank the following for permission to use
photographs included in this book:
W.R. Grace and Son and Peter N. Pruyn: page 66.
Franklyn Holder of Norton's Studio, pages 2, 20, 29 (lower), 31, 34, 48 (upper),
56 (rice paddy), 67 (bottom left and right), 100, 101 (margins), 145 (centre),
149, 156.
Martin Mordecai, pages 26 (margin and bottom), 56 (watercress), 87, 101
(bottom right), 113.
Holt Studios/Primrose Peacock, page 124 (Anglo-Nubian nanny goat).
NHPA, page 124 (Zebu bull, Saanen goat), 145 (top right).
Trip/B. Gibbs, page 124 (Berkshire pig).
Trip/Mike Alkins, page 148.
Bruce Coleman/Jane Burton, page 139.
J. Allan Cash, pages 153

Although we have made every effort to trace and contact all
copyright holders before publication this has not been possible in all
cases. If notified, the publisher will rectify any errors or omissions at
the earliest opportunity.

Contents

Preface

Agricultural Science is an integral component of the curriculum of our primary, junior secondary, composite, senior comprehensive and many senior secondary schools. This three-book series for junior secondary and middle school classes in the Caribbean, has been prepared as an observational/activity-oriented course, and is intended to assist teachers in their agricultural programmes through the encouragement in the pupil of an enquiring and practical attitude toward the subject.

To make the best use of this series it is essential that the teacher should read and study the lessons well in advance so that he/she can prepare the necessary teaching aids and experiments, both of which are vital in the effective teaching of Agricultural Science.

Pupils should be encouraged to investigate and find out more about agriculture in their own localities, and to keep careful records of their findings.

Most of the chapters are designed for teachers to begin their lessons with observations, followed by discussions, inferences, and the application of these inferences in agricultural practices. Practical activity is an essential part of this exercise.

The school garden should be established. This should contain plants and features that can be used for reference and study purposes. Field trips and demonstrations all help to make the teaching programme more effective and stimulating.

Every attempt should be made to integrate the agricultural studies with those of the general science and social studies programmes, as well as any other allied subject in the school curriculum.

Though teachers should find the text adequate, they should feel free to adapt the lesson material to suit their own locality and interest, and to supplement the text with any further reading material that they may consider relevant and helpful.

R.S.P.
October 1993

1 The internal structure of garden plants

Lesson objectives

The plant is made up of several parts. In order to understand how the various parts of the plant carry out the functions they perform it is essential to know more about the internal structures and features of the plant.

On completing this lesson you should be able to:

1 describe the internal structures of the parts of a plant.

2 draw and label the internal structures of the various parts of the plant.

3 state the functions of cells and tissues.

4 describe the process of cell division in plants.

5 explain how plants increase in size and weight during the process of growth.

In the first book of this series we learned about the external features of a plant and their functions. The diagram below will help you to remember the parts of a plant.

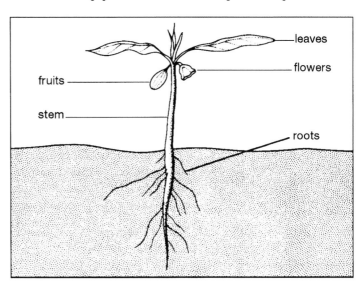

The parts of a plant

In order to understand how the various parts of the plant carry out the functions they perform, you need to know more about the internal structures and features of the plants we grow. Let us look at some of the inner parts of the plant.

Plant cells

Take the thick leaf of an onion and break it. Look at the inside. You cannot see much with your naked eye. To see very small things you need a **microscope**.

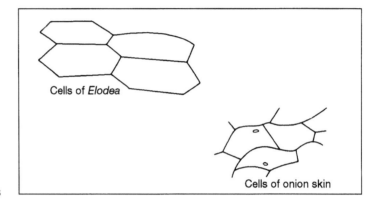

Different types of cells

Now look through a microscope at a thin piece of onion skin or a thin piece of *Elodea* leaf. You will see several tiny structures like the ones in the picture above. These are called cells.

The body of the plant is made up of cells, which may vary in size and shape and in the functions they perform. However, there are some basic properties common to the cells of all plants.

This illustration shows you the general structure of the cell of *Elodea* as seen under the microscope.

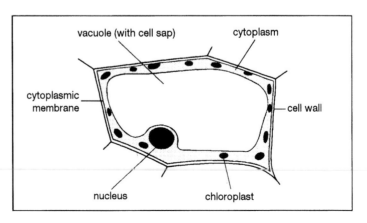

A plant cell

The plant cell consists of four major parts. These are the cell wall, the cytoplasm, the **nucleus**, and the vacuole. The cell wall is made of cellulose. It is permeable, that is, it allows the movement of water into and out of the cell. It also helps to maintain the shape and rigidity of the cell.

The cytoplasm is a jelly-like transparent substance. It may contain particles such as **chloroplasts**, starch granules and fat droplets. In the cytoplasm there are many other specialised parts which perform functions which are essential to the life of the plant.

The nucleus is embedded in the cytoplasm. It is considered the most important part of the cell; without it the cell would die. The nucleus controls the many functions performed by the cell. Cell division takes place only in the presence of the nucleus.

The vacuole is a cavity filled with a fluid called cell sap. The cell sap contains salts, sugars, and other substances dissolved in water. An abundance of cell sap helps to keep the cell in a turgid or swollen state.

Plant tissues

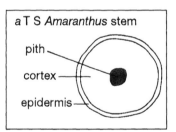

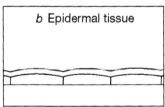

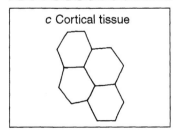

The illustrations on this page show two types of tissue taken from the stem of the *Amaranthus* or bhaji plant.

Plant tissues are made up of groups of cells. These cells are similar in structure, that is, they have the same size, shape and components, and they perform the same functions. Tissues are organised to form organs and systems.

The structure and function of the epidermis

The **epidermis** is made up of regularly-shaped cells which form a protective skin over the plant. Epidermal cells commonly have a protective layer of wax on the outer surface to prevent them losing too much water to the air.

The structure and function of pith

Pith is a cylinder of spongy tissue which lies within the system. It is used for the storage of food.

The structure and function of the cortex

The cortex is a region of spongy cells set between the outer skin and the **vascular tissue**. The cortex helps to keep the stem rigid by pressing out the epidermis.

The structure and functions of vascular tissue

The plant obtains water and mineral salts in solution from the soil by means of its root hairs. These substances are conducted by special xylem tissues to the leaves, where they are used to make plant foods. The products are removed by phloem tissues to other parts of the plant for immediate use or to be stored. The xylem and the phloem tissues together form the vascular system of the plant.

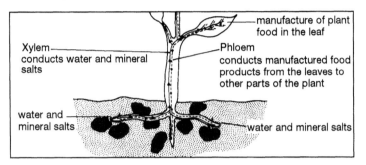

Xylem conducts water and mineral salts

manufacture of plant food in the leaf

Phloem conducts manufactured food products from the leaves to other parts of the plant

water and mineral salts

water and mineral salts

The xylem

The xylem is made up of several components, the chief of which are the xylem vessels. These are large barrel-shaped cells. The protoplasmic mass is destroyed and the end walls break down to form long continuous tubes through which water and other substances can move up to the leaves.

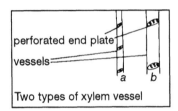

perforated end plate

vessels

a b

Two types of xylem vessel

The phloem

Phloem consists chiefly of sieve elements or sieve tubes. These are cells with sieve-like areas on their end plates and side walls. In these areas the cell protoplasm connects by means of protoplasmic threads. The food materials of the plant are transported through the plant by means of the phloem. These materials finally co-ordinate themselves to form the body of the plant.

This diagram shows how the plant's body is made up.

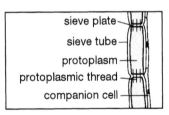

sieve plate

sieve tube

protoplasm

protoplasmic thread

companion cell

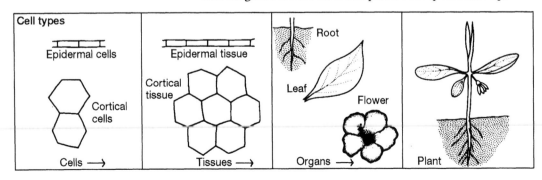

Cell types

Epidermal cells

Cortical cells

Cells →

Epidermal tissue

Cortical tissue

Tissues →

Root

Leaf

Flower

Organs →

Plant

Growth of the plant in size and weight

Look at the growth of the plants in your school compound or home garden. You will observe that as they grow and put out more branches, their roots develop further into the soil. Their stems and branches increase in size and weight. Plants increase in size and weight by increasing their cell size and cell numbers, and by developing new cellular materials. New cells are continually formed by special tissues called **meristems** whose cells divide. These are located at special growing points found in the tips of the roots and shoots.

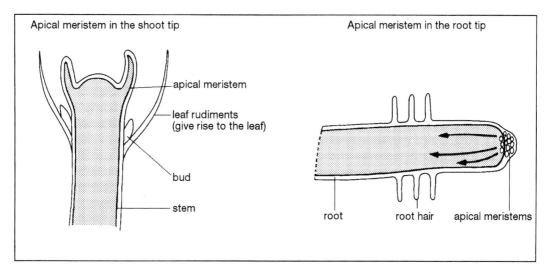

The increase in **girth**, that is, the thickness of the stem or trunk, results from new tissues derived from the **cambium**. The cambium is a ring of meristem which divides, producing phloem cells on the outside of the ring and xylem cells towards the centre.

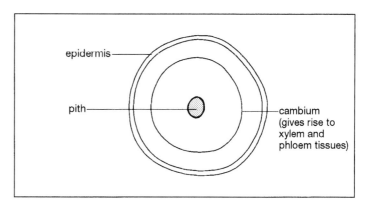

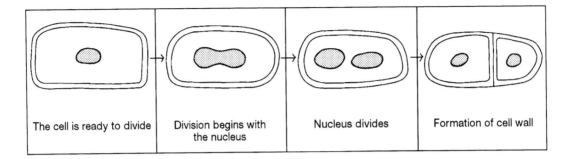

| The cell is ready to divide | Division begins with the nucleus | Nucleus divides | Formation of cell wall |

Cell division in the meristem tissue
New cells are formed in the process of cell division, that is, one cell gives rise to two new cells. The process begins with the splitting of the nucleus and is completed by the formation of a new cell wall laid down by the cytoplasm.

The internal structure of the root

You will remember that the root grows into the soil and its chief functions are to anchor the plant and to obtain water and mineral supplies. Let us look at the internal structure of the root system, which will later help us to understand how some of these root functions are performed.

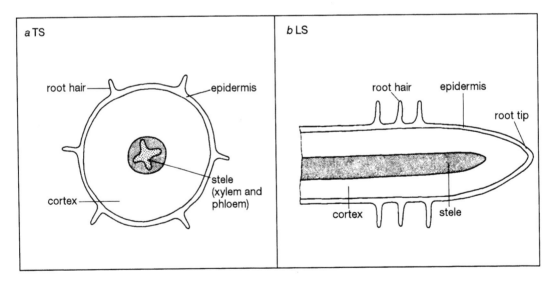

Look through a microscope at the cross sections and vertical sections of the *Amaranthus* or bhaji root. You will see that the tissues are arranged like the ones here.

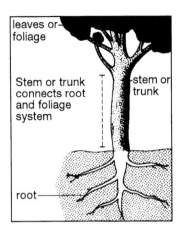

leaves or foliage

Stem or trunk connects root and foliage system

stem or trunk

root

The internal structure of the stem

You will notice that the stem or trunk forms the main connection between the roots of the plant and the foliage above. Stems may perform similar functions, but they often vary in their structure.

Examine a variety of stems and you will observe that they may be soft, woody, fibrous or hollow. The stems of grasses are generally jointed.

Tissues of the stem

The illustrations on this page show you the tissue arrangements of the corn (monocot) and the bean (dicot) stems as seen in transverse section under the microscope.

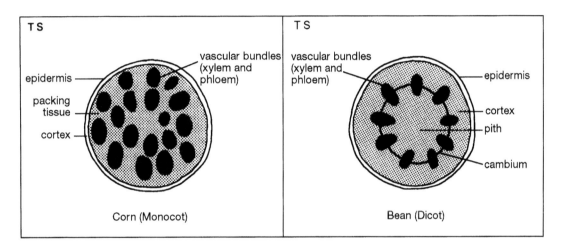

TS

epidermis

packing tissue

cortex

vascular bundles (xylem and phloem)

Corn (Monocot)

TS

vascular bundles (xylem and phloem)

epidermis

cortex

pith

cambium

Bean (Dicot)

The stem is made up of the epidermis, the cortex, the vascular bundles and the pith. The vascular bundles consist of the xylem and the phloem and are derived from the cambium. The arrangement of these tissues differs in monocot and dicot plants.

You will remember that parts of the stem of some plants are eaten as food, for example spinach and sugar cane, whilst the stems of the teak and cedar are used for making lumber.

The internal features of the leaf

We learned in Book 1 that photosynthesis and transpiration take place chiefly in the leaves of plants. Leaves, too, are largely responsible for maintaining the balance of oxygen and carbon dioxide in the atmosphere.

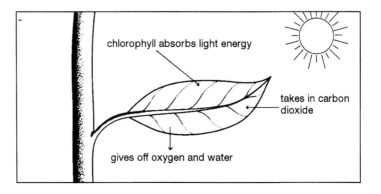

chlorophyll absorbs light energy

takes in carbon dioxide

gives off oxygen and water

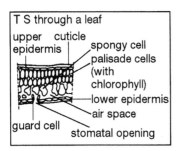

T S through a leaf

upper epidermis   cuticle

spongy cell

palisade cells (with chlorophyll)

lower epidermis

air space

guard cell

stomatal opening

The diagram on the left shows you the internal features of the bean leaf under the microscope. Observe the upper and lower epidermal cells, between which are the closely packed palisade cells, which contain chlorophyll, and the spongy cells, which are loosely packed with air spaces between them. The palisade and spongy tissues together make up the **mesophyll**. On the upper epidermis there is a thin layer of waxy tissue known as the **cuticle**. The lower epidermis, however, is broken by the stomatal openings.

What special functions do the cells with chlorophyll perform?

What is the importance of the stomatal openings in the leaves?

The structure of the fruit

On the next page are pictures of some local fruits. There may be others that you know and which may be abundant in your own country. Make a list of twelve local fruits that are eaten as cooked or uncooked foods, and which may also be used in processing, that is, for making jams, jellies juices and preserves.

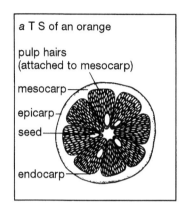

a T S of an orange

pulp hairs
(attached to mesocarp)

mesocarp

epicarp

seed

endocarp

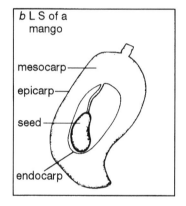

b L S of a
mango

mesocarp

epicarp

seed

endocarp

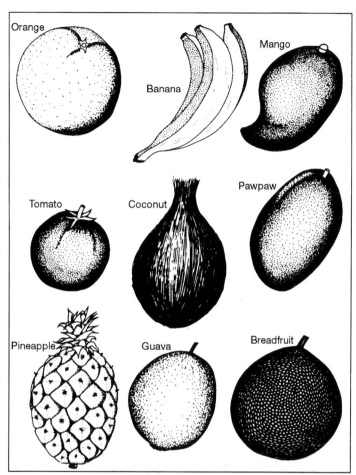

Orange

Banana

Mango

Tomato

Coconut

Pawpaw

Pineapple

Guava

Breadfruit

Fruits vary considerably in their shape, internal structure and chemical composition. The diagrams on the left show you a transverse section of an orange and a longitudinal section of a mango. Get actual specimens and identify the parts shown in the diagrams.

Summary

A knowledge of the internal structures and features of a plant helps us to understand how it carries out the functions it performs. The body of the plant is made up of cells. A cell contains four major parts. These are the cell wall, the cytoplasm, the nucleus and the vacuole. Of these parts, the nucleus is the most important, for without it the cell will die.

Plant tissues are made up of groups of cells that are of the same size, shape and components and perform the same functions. There are several types of plant tissues but the most common ones are the epidermis, the cortex, the vascular bundles and the pith. These tissues are organised to form the various organs and systems of the plant.

Plants increase in size and weight. They do this by increasing their cell size and cell numbers, and by building up new cellular materials. New cells are continually formed by means of cell division from special tissues called 'meristems'. These are usually found at the tips of the shoots and the roots. The increase in girth, however, results from new tissues derived from the cambium.

A tranverse section of the root shows three types of tissues. These are the epidermis, from which the root hairs develop, the cortex and the stele, which consists of the xylem and the phloem. The tissues in the stem are similar to those in the root. The xylem and the phloem, however, are closely associated, and form the vascular bundles. These bundles are arranged differently in monocot and dicot stems.

The leaf is generally thin and has a flat surface. It is made up of an upper and a lower epidermis between which is the mesophyll. This consists of the palisade and the spongy cells. Chloroplast is found mainly in the palisade cells, whilst the stomatal openings are usually found in the lower epidermis.

Fruits vary considerably in their shape and internal structure. For example, a longitudinal section of the mango shows that it is made up of the epicarp, the mesocarp, the endocarp and the seed. Most fruits show these parts, but they may be arranged differently.

Remember these

Cambium Meristematic tissues in the stem which give rise to the vascular bundles.

Chloroplast Particles present in the cytoplasm which give rise to chlorophyll development.

Cuticle A protective layer of waxy tissue on the outer surface of the epidermal cells.

Epidermis The tissue which forms the outer covering of plants.

Girth The circumference or thickness of the shoot of a plant.

Meristems Specialised tissues found at the shoot and root tips and in the cambial region of the stem. Their main function is to produce new cellular materials for shoot and root growth and for the increase in girth.

Mesophyll The layer of palisade and spongy tissues which lie between the upper and lower epidermis of the leaf.

Microscope An instrument which magnifies objects, or makes them look bigger than they are.

Nucleus A component of the cell which is responsible for keeping the cell alive, and for initiating cell division.

Vascular tissue Xylem and phloem tissues which form the conducting elements of plants.

Practical activities

1 Observe the cells of the tomato or cucumber stem under the microscope. Look for the cell wall, the cytoplasm, the vacuole and the nucleus. Draw a diagram and label these parts of the the cell.
2 Collect stems of the following plants: pawpaw, rice, corn, tomato, lettuce, bamboo, sugar cane, orange, elephant grass, bean, mango and coconut. Group them according to the categories below.

Hollow inside	Solid but soft	Solid but fibruous	Solid but woody

3 The illustrations on page 7 show you the tissue arrangement of the corn (monocot) and the bean (dicot) stems as seen under the microscope. Draw and label the diagrams.
4 Examine the transverse section of an orange fruit. Make a drawing and label the internal features. Give examples of two other fruits whose structures look like the orange.
5 Draw a diagram to illustrate the stages in the process of cell division which takes place in meristematic tissues.

Do these test exercises

1 Complete the following sentences by filling in the blank spaces.

a The cell dies in the absence of the ....

b The turgidity of the plant cell is largely controlled by ....

c Movement of water from the roots to the leaves takes place by means of the ....

d Some cells are called meristematic because ....

e Photosynthesis takes place in the palisade cells because ....

2 Select the best answer from the choices given.

a Cellulose is a major component of the:

A cytoplasm

B nucleus

C cell wall

D cell sap

b Cell division begins with the splitting of the:

A nucleus

B chloroplast

C vacuole

D cytoplasm

c The function of the phloem is to:

A transport water from the roots to the leaves.

B control the water requirement of the plant

C produce cellular material to increase the thickness of the stem.

D transport food materials to the various parts of the plant.

d The part labelled 'R' is the:

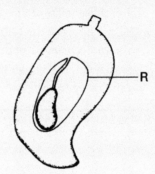

A seed

B endocarp

C epicarp

D mesocarp

e The root hair is a projection of the:

A epidermis

B cortex

C xylem

D phloem

3 Name the major parts of a plant cell. Give a brief description of any two parts named.

4 Name the tissues found in a dicot stem (bean) and state their functions.

5 Say how:

a plants control their water loss on hot days.

b water moves from the soil to the leaves of the plant.

c xylem vessels differ from sieve tubes.

d meristems assist in plant growth.

6 Say why:

a tomatoes grown in the open give higher yields than those grown in the shade.

b a tree that is ring-barked dies.

7 Write a short paragraph saying how nutrition takes place in a plant.

2

The propagation of garden plants by seeds

Lesson objectives

You are going to learn about the propagation of garden plants by seeds. Some seeds can be planted directly in garden plots, others must be sown in a nursery first and then transplanted. This lesson deals mainly with the preparation of seedlings in a nursery. On completing this lesson, you should be able to:

1 state reasons for preparing seedlings in a nursery.

2 list the requirements of a garden nursery.

3 describe the structure of a nursery shed.

4 construct a seed box.

5 list the components of a potting soil.

6 prepare a potting soil.

7 prepare a seed box and a seed bed for sowing seeds.

8 sow seeds and 'thin out' seedlings.

9 care for seedlings in a nursery.

10 'harden off' seedlings in preparation for transplanting.

In Book One we learnt that ornamental and garden plants are propagated sexually by seeds or asexually from other vegetative parts of the plants. In this lesson we are going to learn more about the propagation of plants by seeds.

Looking at seeds

Collect mature seeds from the following plants: corn, melongene, cauliflower, patchoi, bodi-beans and pigeon peas. Observe them carefully. You will notice that seeds vary in colour, size, shape and weight. Some seeds like corn, bodi-beans and pigeon peas are generally planted directly in the garden plot. Others like tobacco, cauliflower and patchoi are sown in a **nursery** and then **transplanted** into the field.

You should now be able to give three reasons why different plants are treated in these different ways.

The garden nursery

Farmer Joe grows tomatoes. His plants bear many large fruits. Do you know why? He plants strong healthy seedlings which are given good care and attention. Let us see how Farmer Joe prepares tomato seedlings in his garden nursery.

This picture shows you Farmer Joe's garden nursery. Look at it carefully and you will notice that it consists of a nursery shed and many boxes of tomato seedlings.

Look at the picture below. Do you know how the farmer uses these pieces of equipment to grow seedlings?

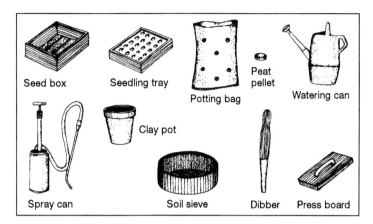

The nursery shed

Look at the nursery shed in this picture. The floor is concreted and the seed boxes are placed on nursery stands above the ground. The clear plastic sheet covering the roof shelters the seedlings from heavy rainfall and allows light to enter the nursery whilst the tall hedge around the shed protects the plants from strong drying winds and straying animals.

Now find answers for these questions.

1 Why is a concrete floor better than a dirt floor?
2 Give two reasons why stands are essential in a nursery shed.
3 How do the sun, the rain, and the wind affect the healthy growth of seedlings?

Containers for sowing seeds

Seeds are usually sown in seed boxes, seedling trays, clay or plastic pots, potting bags or in specially prepared **peat pellets**.

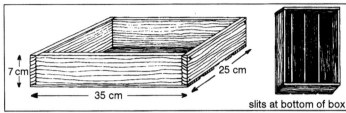
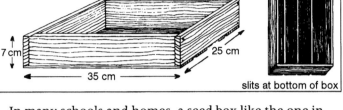

7 cm

25 cm

35 cm

slits at bottom of box

In many schools and homes, a seed box like the one in the picture is used for growing seedlings. A box of this size is light and easy to manage. At the bottom of the box there are slits which allow excess water to drain out. As a result aeration is improved and the plants grow healthily.

How many seedlings could you grow in this box if they were planted 5 cm apart?

Nursery or potting soil

The garden nursery needs a very special soil for the growth of healthy seedlings. A good potting soil provides adequate amounts of **nutrients** (or plant foods). It is well aerated, readily drained and free from disease organisms.

Farmer Joe's potting soil is mixed as in the list above. The contents are thoroughly combined and treated with a soil insecticide. It is then **sterilised** with formaldehyde to control harmful organisms.

1 bucket clay

2 buckets well-rotted compost or pen-manure

2 buckets river-sand

1 bucket coconut bast or peat moss

114 g super phosphate

57 g lime

The treated soil is covered with a plastic sheet for a period of fourteen to twenty-one days, and then aerated for ten to fourteen days before it is used.

Investigate the importance of each component of a good potting soil: (a) clay (b) compost or pen manure (c) river sand (d) coconut bast or peat moss (e) super phosphate (f) lime.

Why should the soil be sterilised and aerated before use?

Preparing a seed box for sowing seeds

A well-prepared seed box contains an adequate amount of soil which is well drained and aerated. The diagram shows you how Farmer Joe prepares his seed box. He places a thin layer of straw at the bottom of the box in order to cover the slits and so prevent the soil from falling through. On this he puts 3.5 to 4 cm of unsifted potting soil. He then fills up the box with finely sifted soil and presses it down gently to a depth of 1–1.5 cm from the top. The box is lightly watered and set aside for sowing seeds.

straw

unsifted potting soil

sifted potting soil

Sowing seeds

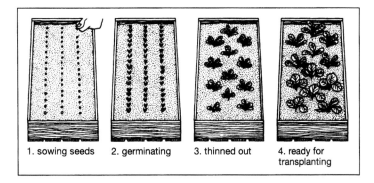

1. sowing seeds   2. germinating   3. thinned out   4. ready for transplanting

Seeds are sown thinly and evenly on the surface, and barely covered with a layer of very fine soil. The box is then covered and placed in a cool sheltered position to await germination.

Some seeds, like those of melongene, hot pepper, and celery, take a long time to germinate. It may be necessary to water them occasionally before germination begins. Seeds of lettuce, patchoi and cabbage germinate within two or three days and need not be watered until after germination. When 70 to 75 per cent of the seeds have germinated, that is, when their radicles appear, the covering should be removed to allow the seedlings to get light.

seed leaf held between the forefinger and the thumb

Thinning out

Would you get healthy, vigorous plants from a box of overcrowded seedlings? **Thinning out** helps to give the seedlings more light and room for root development, and to prevent the incidence of disease.

When two or three leaves are formed, the seedlings should be thinned out. The soil round the root of the plant is stirred and the seedling is held by a leaf, gently lifted, and transplanted into its new box. The seedlings should be 5 cm apart. They are then watered and placed in a cool position.

Remember that seedlings are best thinned out when they are very young. Do you know why? At this stage only a few roots have developed and so the seedlings are removed with little or no root damage.

After-care

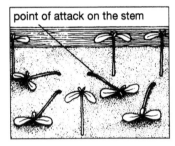

point of attack on the stem

Watering

Why is watering essential? How often should the seedlings be watered? Under moist conditions, roots grow, develop, and absorb nutrients from the soil, so when conditions are dry the plants should be watered once or twice a day. In wet weather, water may be needed every two or three days.

Very damp conditions favour the development of the **'damping off'** fungus. This attacks the stems of the young plants at ground level. The stems rot and the plants fall over and die.

Soil aeration

Heavy rain or constant watering may cause surface crusting. This crust must be broken periodically so as to allow the infiltration of water and exchange of gases.

Weed control

You will remember that weeds compete with cultivated plants for light, water, and nutrient supplies. Seedlings should be kept free from weeds. This is best done by hand-picking the weeds while they are still young and tender.

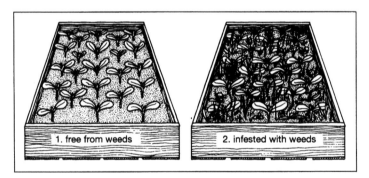

1. free from weeds   2. infested with weeds

Application of fertilisers

In the presence of a well-prepared potting soil there is little or no need for additional fertilisers. However, vegetative growth is helped by the application of a nitrogenous fertiliser like sulphate of ammonia.

A few grains of the fertiliser are sprinkled on the surface of the soil and then watered in. The fertiliser may also be dissolved in water (1 teaspoonful to 4.5 litres of water), and applied as a solution. The fertiliser (or the solution) must not touch the foliage.

Pest and disease control

Look at the seedlings in your garden nursery. You may see leaf and stem damage done by caterpillars or by biting and sucking insects. The leaf miner tunnels between the upper and lower surfaces of the leaf, whilst fungi are mainly responsible for 'damping off' and leaf spot diseases.

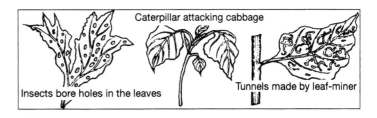

Caterpillar attacking cabbage

Insects bore holes in the leaves

Tunnels made by leaf-miner

Pest and disease control is best achieved by spraying regularly with a chemical mixture consisting of an insecticide, a **fungicide** and a **sticker**, that is, a substance to make the chemical stick to the plant. Your garden shop will supply you with these chemicals.

Hardening off

Seedlings must be planted out in the field as early as possible. During their last two weeks in the nursery they should be exposed to the sun and the rain. This prepares them to stand up to weather conditions in the field.

Seedlings should not be allowed to become overgrown in the nursery. If planted, such seedlings show poor growth and development, and their crop yields are generally low.

Farmer Joe planted a large field of cabbage. He grew cabbage seedlings in a seed bed. Do you know what a seed bed is? It is a small plot (usually raised from the ground) specially prepared for growing seedlings.

The seed bed

Preparation of a seed bed

Select a site in the open field near to the plot where the cabbage is to be planted. Make a raised bank or bed 2 m long and 1 m wide to a height of 20 cm above the ground. On the surface of the bed, spread a 6 cm layer of sifted sterilised potting soil and water gently.

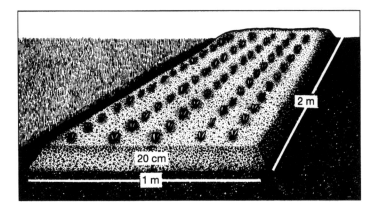

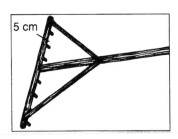

Sowing seeds

Sow the seeds thinly and evenly on the surface of the seed bed and blind with a thin layer of finely sifted soil. The seeds may also be sown in tiny drills that are spaced about 5 cm apart. A row-marker will help to make drills that are uniform in depth and evenly spaced. After sowing, cover the bed with dark sarran netting until germination begins.

After-care

On germination the sarran netting is removed. Under hot or very wet conditions the tender seedlings are protected with a plant protector. As the seedlings grow stronger they should be fully exposed to the weather. Watering, weed control, the application of fertilisers, and spraying against pest and diseases, must be done in the same way as for seedlings grown in seed boxes.

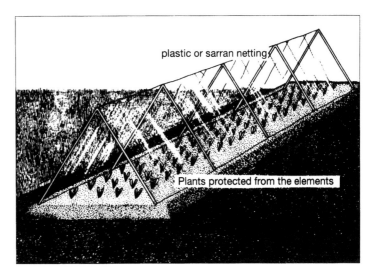

plastic or sarran netting

Plants protected from the elements

Summary

Many ornamental and garden plants are propagated by seeds. Seeds vary in colour, size, shape and weight. Some seeds like corn, bodi-beans and pigeon peas are planted directly in the garden plots. Others like tobacco, cauli-flower and patchoi must be sown in a nursery before being transplanted into the field.

Seedlings are produced in a garden nursery or in a seed bed. The nursery consists of a shed with containers for sowing seeds, well prepared potting soil and other nursery equipment. It is important that the seedlings get adequate amounts of light and are protected from heavy rain and drying winds. The potting soil should provide a good supply of nutrients. It should be well aerated, readily drained and free from disease organisms.

A seed box should be light and easy to manage. The box should be structured to accommodate just as much potting soil as the seedlings and to facilitate drainage. A seed bed, however, is generally used for preparing seedlings on a large scale. The bed is usually raised above ground level and on the surface there is a layer of well prepared potting soil 4 to 6 cm deep.

Seeds should be sown thinly and evenly. They should be slightly covered with fine soil and allowed to germinate. When the seedlings have developed two or three leaves they should be thinned out to a distance of 5 cm apart.

There are several after-care management practices. These include watering, soil aeration, weed control, pest and disease control and the application of fertilisers. About two weeks before transplanting the seedlings are 'hardened off', that is, gradually exposed to full sunshine and heavy rainfall. This prepares them to face weather conditions in the field.

Remember these

'Damping off'	A fungal disease which attacks the stems of young seedlings just above ground level.
Fungicide	A chemical which destroys fungi.
'Hardening off'	The gradual exposure of seedlings to weather conditions in preparation for transplanting into the fields.
Nursery	A place where seedlings are produced.
Nutrients	Mineral substances used as plant foods.
Peat pellet	A small ball of compressed peat moss used in the preparation of seedlings.
Sterilised soil	Soil treated to make it free from disease and other harmful organisms.
Sticker	A substance in a spray mixture which sticks the chemicals to the plants sprayed.
'Thinning out'	The process of spacing out seedlings so as to give them more light and room for root development.
Transplanting	The act of planting out seedlings into their permanent positions in the field.

Practical activities

1 Collect the following seeds and try to find out more about them by completing the table below: tobacco, melongene, tomato, cauliflower, corn, cabbage, celery, pigeon-pea, bodi-bean, patchoi and sorrel.

Seeds	Colour	Shape: rounded or not rounded	Size: large, small, very small	Number of seeds to the gram

Which is the smallest, and which is the largest seed?

Which seeds resemble each other closely? Why?

How does the seed of the tomato differ from that of the pigeon-pea?

What reasons can you give for the difference in the number of seeds to the gram?

Which seeds could safely be planted directly into the garden plot?

Which seeds should be sown in a nursery and then transplanted?

Why do they need this treatment?

2 Construct a seed box like the one on page 16 and prepare it for sowing lettuce seeds.

Sow patchoi or mustard seeds in the soil-types listed in the table below. Water them regularly and keep them free from weeds. At the end of three weeks make observations on the growth of the plants in the various soil-types. Give reasons for the observations made. Say which is the best soil type for seedlings and explain why.

Soil-type	Observation on growth of plants	Reasons
River sand		
Clay		
Compost or pen manure		
Potting soil		

3 Grow seedlings of tomato, patchoi, cabbage, lettuce, sweet-pepper and celery in your school nursery.

Complete the observations in the table below.

Seeds	Date sown	Date germinated	Date thinned out	Date transplanted into garden plot
Tomato				
Patchoi				
Lettuce				
Cabbage				
Sweet-pepper				
Celery				

Say how the observations in this table are useful to a farmer.

Do these test exercises:

1 Consider these statements carefully. State whether they are *true* or *false*.

a 'Hardening off' prepares seedlings to withstand weather conditions in the field.

b Sulphate of ammonia is a fertiliser rich in nitrogen.

c In the process of germination the plumule appears before the radicle.

d The addition of peat moss to a potting soil helps it to retain water.

e 'Damping off' disease is more prevalent under dry conditions than under wet conditions.

2 In parts a–d select the best answer from the choices given.

a Which plant has the smallest seed?

A patchoi
B cauliflower
C tobacco
D sweet pepper

b The group of seeds that is best suited for direct planting in the field is:

A ochro, bodi-beans, corn
B cauliflower, tomato, melongene
C sweet pepper, cabbage, celery
D celery, patchoi, tomato

c The correct order of operation in preparing a seed box is:

A coarse soil, straw, fine soil, gentle watering
B fine soil, straw, coarse soil, gentle watering
C straw, fine soil, coarse soil, gentle watering
D straw, coarse soil, fine soil, gentle watering

d Which component should be added to a potting soil to improve drainage?

A pen manure
B clay
C river sand
D peat moss

e The process of 'thinning out'

(i) enables seedlings to get more light.
(ii) gives seedlings more room for root development
(iii) increases the incidence of diseases

Which of the above statements are correct?

A (i) and (ii)
B (i) and (iii)
C (ii) and (iii)
D (i), (ii) and (iii)

3 State why:

a shallow seed boxes are better for growing seedlings than deep boxes

b seeds should be sown evenly and thinly

c slits are necessary at the bottom of a seed box

d a farmer usually sows more seeds than his field plot requires

4 Explain why

a the roof of a nursery shed should be made of clear plastic

b potting soil is sterilised.

c seeds of melongene and sweet pepper take a longer time to germinate than those of cabbage and lettuce

d seedlings should be 'thinned out' in their early stages of growth

5 Describe how you would

a prepare a seed box for sowing seeds

b sow patchoi seeds

6 Give three examples in each case of seeds which are:

a planted directly in the garden plot.

b first sown in nurseries and then transplanted.

Give reasons for the examples you have chosen

7 Describe how you would care for a box of tomato or sweet pepper seedlings from the time of sowing seeds till the plants are ready for transplanting.

3

The cultivation of vegetable crops

Lesson objectives

Many farmers engage themselves in the production of short term vegetable crops such as tomatoes, beans, lettuce and carrots. These crops have specific requirements and production practices.

At the end of this lesson you should be able to:

1 explain the concept of 'short term vegetable crops'.

2 prepare a list of vegetable crops with the popular varieties in production.

3 prepare land for the cultivation of a named vegetable crop.

4 line and stake out a plot for planting.

5 transplant seedlings in the field.

6 care for crops after planting out.

7 perform simple experiments related to the use of manures, fertilisers and chemical sprays.

8 harvest crops at the proper stage of maturity.

9 apply post harvest treatment.

Mr Kumar grows **short-term** vegetable crops, that is, crops which grow and bear within a short period of time. The crops he cultivates are mainly tomatoes, beans, lettuce and carrots. These are all grown and harvested within a period of three to four months.

Let us see how farmer Kumar cultivates these crops.

Farmer Kumar tends his crops

The tomato

Tomato plants on stakes

Varieties

Farmer Kumar grows tomatoes on a large scale. He selects those varieties which are high yielding, disease resistant and best suited for cropping all the year round. The main varieties that he cultivates are the *Early Cascade*, the *Calypso*, the *Nema* and the *Capitan*. He also cultivates the *Red Rock*, the *Oxheart* and the local dwarf varieties, but these latter varieties are better suited to the dry season.

Tomato seedlings planted out

Soil and land preparation

Tomatoes can grow on a wide range of soil types. However, they thrive best on light, free-draining loamy soils.

Farmer Kumar ploughs and rotavates the soil, and enriches it by incorporating pen-manure or **artificial fertilisers** (such as NPK). Mole crickets and cutworms are destroyed by spraying the soil with a **soil insecticide**. In the wet season the farmer grows his tomatoes on raised beds or banks. This helps to remove excess soil water which may be harmful to the roots of the plants.

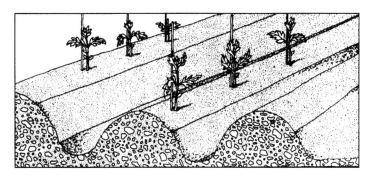

Tomatoes growing on raised beds

Planting material

Seeds are sown in seed-boxes to a depth of 3 mm. After germination, the seedlings are thinned out to 5 cm apart, and are allowed to grow for three to four weeks, when they will be ready for transplanting into the field.

Farmer Kumar grows strong, healthy seedlings by ensuring that they are watered regularly, kept free from weeds, fertilised, and sprayed against insect attack and diseases.

Planting and spacing

Seedlings are planted in rows 60 cm apart and with 38 cm between the plants. The plants are taken out with soil attached to the roots and placed in little holes in the garden beds. The soil is pulled gently but firmly around the roots and the plants are then watered. Transplanting is best done in the late afternoon when the weather is cool.

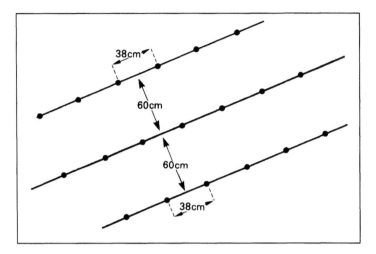

After-care
Farmer Kumar wants a high yielding, good quality crop. He gives his plants considerable care and attention.

Watering
Tomatoes need a regular supply of soil water. In the dry season, water is conserved and maintained in the soil by means of irrigation and **surface mulching**. In the wet season this is probably not necessary.

Weed control
Weeds compete with cultivated plants for soil water, nutrients, and light. In the early stages of tomato growth, Farmer Kumar controls weeds by hoeing. Later, he hoes out the weeds that are about 15–20 cm around the plants and destroys the rest with a herbicide, such as *Gramoxone*, sprayed with a sprayer, using a shield.

Moulding, staking, and pruning
Look at some dwarf varieties of tomato. These tend to grow along the ground. You will notice the growth of adventitious roots from the stem. Farmer Kumar encourages the development of these roots by **moulding**, that is, by pulling soil around the stem of the plant. How does moulding help the plant to grow and bear better fruit?

A farmer plants out seedlings

Tall or medium varieties of tomato must be staked to keep the fruit off the ground and to prevent them from rotting. Pruning is avoided, as this may reduce yields. Sometimes the farmer may stake and prune his plants, allowing only one or two stems to develop. As a result he gets very large fruit, though his yields may be lower.

Fertiliser treatment

Tomatoes are heavy feeders. Farmer Kumar applies a liquid nitrogenous fertiliser at planting time and again six weeks later. At the formation of the second thrust, that is, the second bunch of flowers, the farmer applies a fertiliser rich in potash (13.13.20). Each plant is given about 28 g of fertiliser. Subsequent fertiliser dressings of a similar type are given every 20 to 21 days.

Pest and disease control

Tomatoes are attacked by several pests and diseases. Mole crickets and cutworms are controlled by spraying with a soil insecticide. Leaf-cutting caterpillars and leaf miners are sprayed with *Malathion*.

Where nematodes are prevalent, the soil should be fumigated with formaldehyde before planting.

Leaf blights are rampant during the wet season. These are best controlled by spraying with a copper fungicide such as *Kocide*.

Farmer Kumar uses chemicals with great care. He reads and follows carefully the directions on the labels. Certain chemicals, if not used properly, can be very dangerous.

Harvest and yield

Harvesting of fruit begins by the tenth to fourteenth week after planting. They are best harvested at the mature green stage, or just as soon as they begin to turn red. Harvesting should always be done on bright sunny days.

The fruit should be picked with the calyx on, gently packed in shallow boxes, and placed in a cool open space to ripen. Scarred or damaged fruits should be discarded. Farmer Kumar harvests as much as 22 500–24 000 kg of tomatoes to the hectare.

The tomato as a food

The tomato is a popular fruit in every kitchen. As a food it is especially rich in Vitamins A and C. Find out (a) four ways in which fresh tomatoes are used as food, and (b) five manufactured food products made from tomatoes.

Beans

You will remember that the bean belongs to the family of plants called legumes. These plants enrich the soil by adding nitrogen to it. The beans are rich in protein, an essential food nutrient in human and animal nutrition.

There are many types of bean. However, Farmer Kumar grows 'string beans', also known as 'snap beans'. The pods of these beans are cooked and eaten in the young green stage because they are juicy and have good food value.

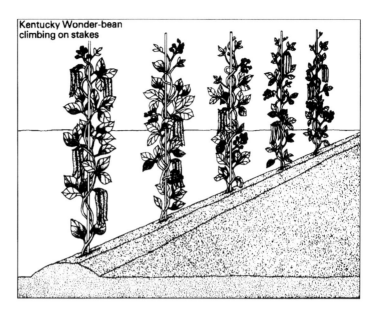

Kentucky Wonder-bean climbing on stakes

Varieties

The pictures on this page show you two varieties of string beans. Some beans like *Kentucky Wonder* or *Blue Lake* are climbers and must be staked. Others like the *Contender Bush* or *Harvester* are dwarf types.

Mr Kumar cultivates the dwarf varieties. What reasons can you give for his choice?

Soil preparation

Beans grow well on loams and clays. The soil must be tilled, drained, and well manured. The plants do not grow well on acid soils, as these prevent the activities of the nodule-forming bacteria. Acid soils should be corrected by the addition of lime.

Planting material

Seeds are taken from freshly collected mature pods. They should be free from disease and physical damage and treated against fungal infection with a fungicide like *Captan*.

Planting and spacing

Seeds are sown directly in the garden plot. Planting distances for dwarf and climbing varieties are shown below. Climbers should be planted in double rows.

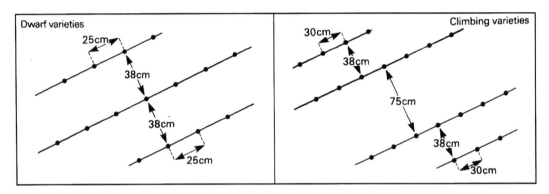

After-care

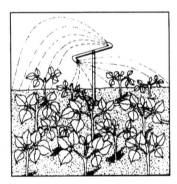

Watering

Some bean varieties need large quantities of water, whilst others can grow under fairly dry conditions. However, even in the latter case, irrigation may be necessary during dry spells or periods of drought.

Weed control

Farmer Kumar sprays his bean plots with a **pre-emergent herbicide**. The soil is sprayed before weed growth begins and before bean seeds germinate. The herbicide delays the germination of the weed seeds, but it has no effect on the bean seeds.

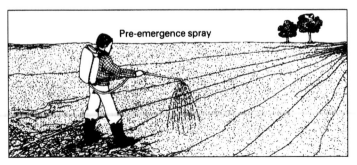

Fertiliser treatment

Beans require good supplies of nitrogen, phosphate and potash. On rich soils the application of nitrogen may not be necessary. Can you tell why? Farmer Kumar applies small quantities of mixed fertiliser every two weeks after sowing until flowering begins.

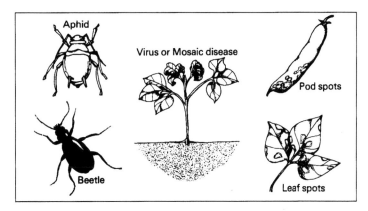

Pest and disease control

Beans are attacked chiefly by aphids, beetles, red-spider, mites, and bean flies. These pests are readily controlled by spraying with an insecticide like *Malathion*.

Lead spots, pod spots, and rusts are fungal diseases. Applying copper and sulphur fungicides helps to control them.

Mosaic or virus diseases can be prevented by planting disease-free material. The picture shows you what a virus-infected plant looks like. Notice the stunted growth. The leaves are smaller, crinkled, and mottled with yellow.

Harvest and yield

Pods are ready for harvesting at six to eight weeks after planting. They are removed from the plant while they are at the snap-stage, that is, at the stage at which the pods snap or break quite easily. Farmer Kumar gets yields as high as 22 000–25 000 kg of beans to the hectare.

Beans as a food

Beans are very rich in vegetable protein and calcium. They also have small quantities of iron and carbohydrate. Why would you include quantities of beans in the diet of vegetarians (people who do not eat meat, fish, or eggs)?

Lettuce

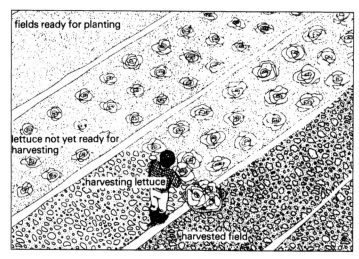

Farmer Kumar is busy at work on his lettuce plot. He has prepared a plot for planting, whilst some of his plots are ready for harvesting. Farmer Kumar grows greater quantities of lettuce in the dry season than in the wet season. This is because heavy rains in the wet season tend to soak and damage the lettuce leaves.

Varieties

There are many varieties of lettuce. Some are *Minetto, Mignonette, Great Lakes, Iceberg* and the *Big Boston*. Farmer Kumar cultivates mainly the *Minetto* and the *Green Mignonette* (photographs on the left). These are vigorous and fast growing, and can be grown under fairly wet conditions. They are popular in the local markets because of their large crisp leaves.

Soil and land preparation

Lettuce will grow on soils which range from sandy loams to clays. The soil should be well tilled, well manured, and well drained. Mixed fertiliser (22.11.11) should be broadcast on the soil about 8–10 days before planting.

Planting material

Seeds are sown in seed-boxes. After germination the seedlings are thinned out to a distance of 5 cm apart.

Seedlings should be kept free from weeds and watered regularly. A liquid application of 28 g of sulphate of ammonia in 4 litres of water, once a week, helps to grow vigorous plants. Protection from hot sun and heavy rain is essential. Seedlings are ready for transplanting when they are 5–7 cm tall.

Transplanting seedlings

Planting and spacing

Seedlings are planted in rows 38–46 cm apart, with 25–30 cm between plants in the row. Greater planting distances are better suited for heavily manured soils.

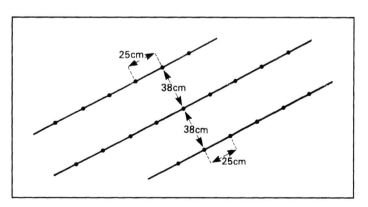

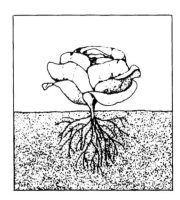

Lettuce root system

After-care

Watering

Regular watering and mulching is essential in the dry season. You will notice that lettuce has a very shallow root system and water shortage could seriously affect its growth. In the *Green Mignonette* type, water deficiency is indicated by a severe browning of the leaves and by a reduction in head size.

Weed control

The plot must be kept free from weeds at all times, by hand picking them when they are young and tender.

Soil aeration

The soil must be kept well aerated, especially during the wet season. Heavy showers of rain tend to cause compaction and surface crusting.

Farmer Kumar uses a hand fork to loosen the soil. In doing this he ensures that soil does not get into the heart of the lettuce, as this may cause the plant to rot.

Fertiliser treatment

A week after planting, Farmer Kumar applies about 14 g of sulphate of ammonia to each plant as a surface dressing. Further applications are made every 14 to 21 days. Sulphate of ammonia is a good fertiliser for lettuce. It is rich in nitrogen, an element which promotes growth in plants.

Pest and disease control

Lettuce is attacked chiefly by aphids, and also by caterpillars of moths and butterflies. These are readily controlled by an insecticide such as *Malathion*.

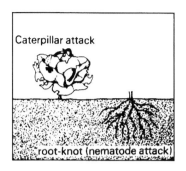

The root-knot nematode damages the root system of the plant and prevents the absorption of nutrients. To control this, the soil should be sprayed with a **nematicide** prior to planting. Crop rotation should also be practised.

Heart rot (decay of the inner leaves) is usually caused by close planting and high fertiliser treatment. Farmer Kumar prevents the occurrence of this disease by making sure that his planting distances and fertiliser treatments are correct.

Harvest and yield

Lettuce is harvested about five to seven weeks after planting. The plants are uprooted carefully and cleaned by removing the roots and old leaves. Any dirt present is washed off and the heads are packed gently in shallow trays or baskets with their cut stems facing upwards. Each head weighs 400–500 g and the yield per hectare is 10 000–12 500 kg.

Lettuce as a food

Lettuce has high levels of calcium and Vitamins A and C. It is eaten uncooked and is used chiefly for making salads. Why is lettuce eaten uncooked?

Carrots

root-tuber

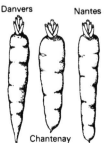

Danvers   Nantes

Chantenay

The carrot is a vegetable root tuber, unlike the cassava which is starchy. Carrots are grown in small quantities for home consumption in many of the Caribbean islands. However, commercial production for the Caricom market has been taking place on the island of St Vincent. Find out why carrots grow well in certain parts of that island.

Varieties

There are several varieties of carrot. The chief variety grown by Farmer Kumar is *Danvers Half Long*. Sometimes he grows *Chantenay* or *Nantes*. The pictures on this page show you what the root tubers of these varieties look like.

Soil preparation

Carrots grow best on light loams or sandy soils rich in **organic matter**. The soil should be ploughed and rotavated to a fine tilth about 23–25 cm deep. Narrow ridges are made at a distance of 90 cm apart from centre to centre. Large quantities of pen manure should not be applied to

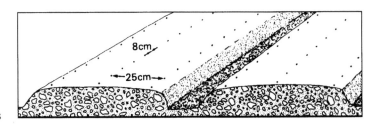

Soil preparation for carrots

the soil as this tends to promote leafy growth at the expense of tuber development.

Planting materials

Plants are grown from seeds. Seeds should be stored in a desiccator as they tend to lose their viability – that is, their ability to grow – very quickly.

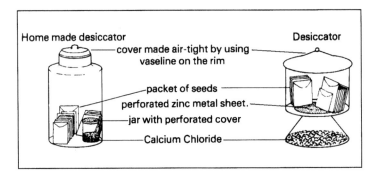

Sowing and spacing

Seeds are mixed with sand to ensure even distribution. They are sown in drills 1.5 cm deep on the ridges. The drills are spaced 25 cm apart. Plants are thinned out to 8 cm apart when they are about 8–10 cm high. When the plants are thinned the remaining plant should be held down firmly whilst the unwanted ones are pulled out. Carrots should not be transplanted. Can you say why?

After-care

Watering and weed control
Irrigation is necessary, especially during the dry season. Weeds are best controlled by the use of a pre-emergent herbicide or by hand-weeding in the early stages of weed growth.

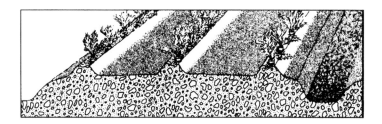

Earthing up

The plant should be earthed up, that is, the earth pulled around the roots, as soon as root growth takes place. This encourages the development of the tubers and protects them from exposure to the light. Light stimulates the development of chlorophyll, which discolours the tuber.

Fertiliser treatment

A mixed fertiliser (10.15.10) is worked into the soil just before the ridges are formed. When the plants are 15 cm high, applications of potash are made every 14 to 21 days. Farmer Kumar is cautious about the heavy application of nitrogen to his carrot crop.

Study this diagram in relationship to nitrogen application, and try to find out the following:
On which soil do carrots show better foliage development?
On which soil does better tuber development take place?

You will notice that nitrogen promotes vegetative growth but root and tuber development are poor.

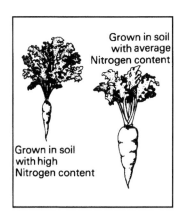

Grown in soil with average Nitrogen content

Grown in soil with high Nitrogen content

Pests and diseases

Carrots are attacked by leaf-cutting insects, such as caterpillars, cutworms and flea-beetles. These insects are controlled by *Sevin* or *Malathion*. Mole crickets and other soil pests are destroyed by a soil insecticide.

'Damping off' may be prevalent under wet conditions and is best controlled by early thinning out and good drainage. Copper fungicides reduce the incidence of blights and leaf spots.

Eelworms or nematodes may be abundant in some soils. These are controlled by treating the soil with a nematicide such as *Nemagon*. Good rotational practices also assist in their control.

Harvest and yield

Roots are ready for harvesting by the twelfth week after sowing. Farmer Kumar uses a fork to lift the tubers and he ensures that they are not damaged or broken. The tops are trimmed and the roots are washed and spread to dry in the open shade.

The tubers are then packed in plastic bags or in crates, and marketed. Tubers that are to be kept for a long time should be refrigerated. Farmer Kumar gets yields as high as 17 500 kg–25 000 kg to the hectare.

Carrots as a food

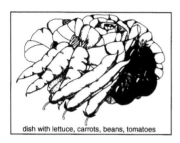
dish with lettuce, carrots, beans, tomatoes

Observe the yellow colour of the carrot root tuber. Did you know that yellow-coloured foods are rich in Vitamin A? Carrots have high Vitamin A and calcium content.

Look at these pictures and make a list of the number of ways in which carrots are used and stored as foods. You may add more to this list.

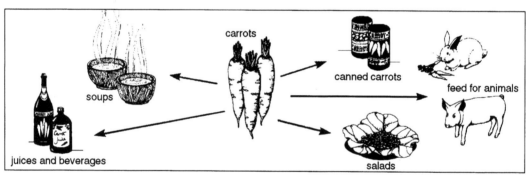

carrots

canned carrots

feed for animals

soups

juices and beverages

salads

Summary

We have seen how farmer Kumar cultivates tomatoes, beans, lettuce and carrots. These crops show considerable variations in their soil and nutrient requirements and in their production practices. The farmer must have a knowledge of the specific requirements and conditions necessary for the production of each crop in order to obtain high yields and good quality products from them.

Crops vary in their soil and nutrient requirements, and in their production practices. The selection of suitable varieties for high yields, disease resistance and for seasonal or all-year production is also very important.

Tomatoes may be cultivated all year round using the *Early Cascade* and the *Calypso* types or mainly in the dry season using the *Red Rock* and the local dwarf varieties. Several other varieties are found in the Caribbean.

Tomatoes grow best on a light, free-draining, loamy soil. Seedlings are prepared in a nursery and transplanted in the field in rows 60 cm apart and with 38 cm between plants in the rows. After-care includes watering, weed control, moulding, staking and pruning, fertiliser treatment and the control of pests and diseases.

Harvesting begins by the tenth to fourteenth week after planting. The crop yield ranges from 22 500 to 24 000 kg per hectare.

As a food, tomato is rich in Vitamins A and C. String beans are grown mostly for their green pods. *Harvester* and *Contender* are the varieties most commonly grown. The crop grows well on loams and clays that are tilled, drained and well manured. Seeds are planted directly in the field plots in rows 38 cm apart and with 25 cm between plants in the rows. After-care includes watering, weed control, fertiliser application and the control of insect pests and diseases.

Pods can be harvested at six to eight weeks after planting. Yields range from 22 000 to 25 000 kg per hectare.

Beans are rich in vegetable proteins and calcium. They are essential in the diets of man and animals.

Beans are also important in crop rotation programmes. They add nitrogen to the soil, making it more fertile.

Lettuce is a leaf crop used mainly in salads. It is rich in calcium and vitamins A and C.

The varieties of lettuce popularly grown are *Mignonette*, *Minetto* and *Iceberg*. The crop can be grown on a wide range of soil types. The land should be well tilled, drained and manured. Seedlings are prepared in nurseries and transplanted when they are about 7 cm tall. Plants are spaced in rows 38–46 cm apart and 25 to 30 cm between plants in the rows. After-care includes watering, weed control, soil aeration, treatment with nitrogenous fertilisers and pest and disease control. The crop can be harvested 5–8 weeks after planting. The yield is 10 000 to 12 500 kg per hectare.

Carrots have vegetable root tubers grown mainly for home consumption. The chief varieties cultivated are *Danver's Half Long*, *Chantenay* and *Nantes*. Carrots grow best on light loams or sandy soils rich in organic matter. Pen or farmyard manures should be avoided. Ridges are made and seeds are sown to a depth of 1.5 cm in drills spaced 25 cm apart on the ridges. Plants are thinned out to 8 cm apart when they are about 8–10 cm high. After-care exercises involve watering and weed control, earthing up, fertiliser treatment, and pest and disease control.

Harvesting of tubers begins by the twelfth week after sowing. The yield ranges from 17 500 to 25 000 kg per hectare.

As a food, carrots are rich in Vitamin A and calcium.

Remember these

Artificial fertiliser	Fertilisers that are manufactured or obtained directly from mineral rocks.
Liquid fertilisers	Fertilisers prepared as solutions before application.
Mixed fertilisers	Fertilisers containing the three major nutrient elements of nitrogen, phosphorus and potassium (N.P.K.).
Moulding	The act of drawing surface soil or placing organic materials around the roots of plants.
Nematicide	A chemical which destroys nematodes.
Organic matter	Substances derived from plant and animals remains.
Pre-emergent herbicide	A herbicide which delays the growth of weeds but has no effect on the germination and growth of the seeds of the cultivated crop.
Short-term crops	Crops which grow and bear within three to four months.
Soil insecticide	A chemical which destroys insects present in the soil.
Surface mulching	A dressing of organic materials placed on the surface of the soil to conserve soil water.

Practical activities

1 Select a plot in your school garden prepared for growing tomatoes.
  a Line and stake out for planting at a distance of 60 cm between rows and 38 cm within the row.
  b Select suitable tomato seedlings and plant out the plot lined and staked in (a) above.
2 Prepare three pots or containers of the same size for growing lettuce and label them L1, L2 and L3.
  In L1 place potting soil that is prepared for sowing seedlings.
  In L2 and L3 place a loam soil to which nothing is added. Plant out the pots with lettuce seedlings that are of the same variety, age and size. Water the plants regularly, aerate the soil and control insect pests. To L2 alone give

100 cc of a liquid fertiliser treatment (7 g sulphate of ammonia to 1 litre of water) once per week.

At the end of the 4th week make the following observations on the growth of the plants.

Pots	Observations	
	Size of plant	Colour of leaves
L1		
L2		
L3		

Give reasons for the differences observed in lettuce growth in the pots L1, L2 and L3.

3 Grow two plots of carrot. Label the plots C1 and C2.

Grow C1 on a sandy loam with nothing added.

Grow C2 on a sandy loam with pen manure added.

Give both plots the same after-care and management. At the end of the 10th week answer the following.

a Which plot showed better shoot growth? Why?

b Which plot showed better tuber development? Why?

c State whether it is advisable to incorporate pen manure in the preparation of plots for growing carrots.

4 Grow two plots of patchoi. Label them P1 and P2. Give the patchoi on both plots the same care and management practices except for insect pest control.

In P1 spray to control insect pests.

In P2 use no sprays.

At the end of the 3rd week after planting, make the following observations.

a Were the plots attacked by insects?

b If there were insect attacks, which plot showed higher levels of attacks?

c State the nature of the attack on the plants.

d Would you advise a farmer to spray his patchoi crop against insect attack? Give reasons for your answer.

5 Here is a list of vegetable crops that could be grown in your school garden: cabbage, cauliflower, cucumber, ochro, tomato, melongene, bean, sweet pepper, carrot, radish, lettuce. Go to a garden shop and find out the varieties that are available. Enter them in a table with these headings.

Vegetable crops	Available varieties

6 Grow any one of the four crops you studied in this lesson. On a large sheet of paper copy out and complete the chart shown below.

Name of crop	Variety	Date planted and planting material	Soil and land preparation	Care during growth	Date harvested and yield	Additional comments

Do these test exercises

1 Select the best answer from the choices given.

a Which of these is a variety of bean?

A Early Cascade

B Nantes

C Harvester

D Minetto

b The most suitable planting distance between rows and within rows for tomatoes is:

A 80 cm between and 60 cm within

B 60 cm between and 38 cm within

C 40 cm between and 32 cm within

D 30 cm between and 25 cm within

c A lettuce crop in its third week of growth should be treated with a fertiliser high in:

A nitrogen

B phosphorus

C potassium

D calcium

d The incorporation of pen-manure in land preparation is NOT recommended in the production of:

A tomato

B lettuce

C bean

D carrot

e 'Earthing up' is a desirable cultivation practice in carrot production. This helps to:

(i) reduce the incidence of diseases.

(ii) encourage tuber development.

(iii) prevent discoloration of the tubers.

Which of the statements above are correct about 'earthing up'?

A (i) and (ii)

B (i) and (iii)

C (ii) and (iii)

D (i), (ii) and (iii)

2 In your own words explain what you understand by:

a Short-term crops.

b Carrot seed loses its viability very quickly.

c A surface dressing of sulphate of ammonia.

3 List the production practices involved in growing a crop of lettuce.

4 Say why:

a Carrots should not be transplanted.

b Better heads of lettuce are obtained in the dry season than in the wet season.

c Beans do not thrive well in acid soils.

5 Give good reasons for:

a Moulding and staking tomatoes.

b Transplanting seedlings in the late afternoon.

c Destroying weeds in their early stages of growth.

d Including beans in the diet of vegetarians.

6 State how you would recognise:

a Virus attack in beans.

b Leaf-miner in tomatoes.

c Nematode attack in lettuce.

d Water shortage in *Green Mignonette* lettuce.

7 Describe how a farmer harvests and prepares the following crops for the market:

a tomatoes

b lettuce

c carrots

4 Rotation of crops

Lesson objectives

Crop rotation is a desirable agricultural practice. Farmers should be acquainted with the principles involved in planning a crop rotation programme and the benefits that are gained by rotating crops.

On completing this lesson you should be able to:

1 define the term 'crop rotation'.

2 explain the principles of crop rotation.

3 list the advantages of crop rotation.

4 plan a crop rotation programme.

5 practise crop rotation in the home and school garden.

6 make observations in connection with crop rotation.

In Chapter 2 we learned that the tomato is grown for its fruits, lettuce for its leaves, carrot for its root and legumes such as beans for their **nitrogen** and protein values. Farmer Kumar rotates these crops, that is, he does not grow the same crop on the same plot all the time. The diagram below shows you how the farmer rotates his crops. Notice the sequence in which the crops are grown.

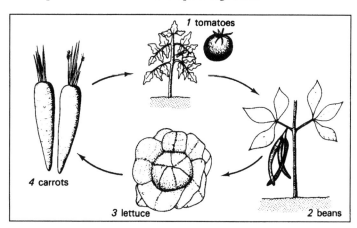

Crop rotation is a useful agricultural practice. It helps to improve and maintain soil fertility and to make better use of soil **nutrients**. It also assists in controlling weeds, insect pests and diseases. As a result, good yields of high quality crops are obtained. The farmer is kept busy all the year round, since his garden is always under cultivation.

Let us study the features of some crops and try to find out what principles are involved in crop rotation and the benefits that are gained by rotating crops.

Take a garden fork and dig out a tomato and a lettuce plant from your home or school garden. Wash the soil from the roots under a tap. Ensure that the roots are not damaged. Study the root systems and find out the following:
Which crop is (a) deep-rooted, (b) shallow-rooted, (c) a surface-feeder, (d) a deep-feeder?

From your observations you will notice that the tomato plant is deep-rooted and obtains its nutrient supplies at a deeper level in the soil than the lettuce which is shallow-rooted and a surface feeder. By rotating a deep rooted crop with a shallow-rooted one, full use is made of the nutrients present at varying levels in the soil.

Crops vary in their nutrient requirements. For example, leaf crops like lettuce and cabbage require large quantities of nitrogen to promote leaf growth, whilst carrot and other root crops need **phosphates** for tuber development.

Rotating a leaf crop with a root crop helps to make maximum and efficient use of the nitrogen and the phosphate present in the soil.

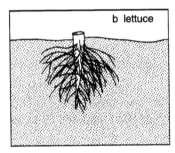

a tomato

b lettuce

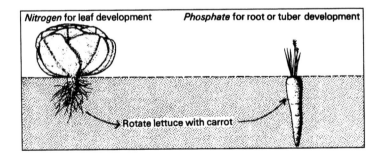

Nitrogen for leaf development   *Phosphate* for root or tuber development

Rotate lettuce with carrot

The soil is the chief medium in which plants grow and it is important to improve and maintain its fertility. A fertile soil is one that is well drained, well aerated and rich in nutrient supplies. It must also be free from harmful organisms and **toxic substances**.

Farmer Kumar knows that some crops like lettuce and corn exhaust the soil of its nitrogen supplies, while others like beans (legumes) add nitrogen instead. In his rotation programme he ensures that a legume crop is followed by a leaf crop. What reason can you give for this?

When grasses are used in a rotation system, their roots decompose to increase soil organic matter and improve soil structure. The decomposed roots leave soil channels which facilitate the movement of air and water in the soil.

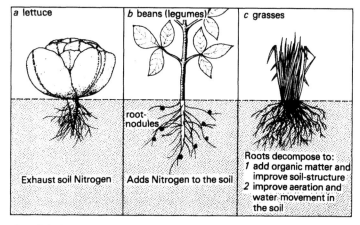

Good **drainage** improves **aeration** and prevents the accumulation of toxic substances in the soil. A well aerated soil is essential for root growth and the development of useful soil organisms.

Farmer Kumar practises crop rotation as a means of controlling pests and diseases in his crops. The table below indicates the pests and diseases which attack crops.

Crops	Pests and diseases
Tomato	Mole crickets, cut worms, caterpillars, leaf miners, leaf blights, nematodes.
Bean	Aphids, beetles, red spider, mites, bean flies, leaf spots, pod spots, rusts.
Lettuce	Aphids, caterpillars, nematodes
Carrot	Leaf-cutting caterpillars, cutworms, flea beetle, mole crickets, nematodes

Study the table and answer these questions.

Are all the crops attacked by the same pests and diseases? Is there a pest or disease which attacks all the crops?

Name a pest or disease which attacks two or more crops. Snap beans and red kidney beans are attacked by the same type of leaf spot diseases. Why is this?

You will notice that some pests and diseases may be common to two or more crops, but all crops are not attacked by the same. On the other hand, crops belonging to the same family are generally attacked by the same types of pests and diseases. In a rotation, pests and diseases do not get a chance to build up, as different crops are attacked by different types.

Crop rotation helps to control weeds. In a rotation system the land has to be ploughed and prepared for each new crop. In the process, weeds are destroyed and turned into the soil to add to its organic content.

Crops infested by weeds

Where the **planting distances** of crops are far apart, as with tomato plants, weeds get an opportunity to compete with the cultivated plants. With beans, however, the planting distance is closer. The plants grow dense **foliage**, cover the ground completely, and outstrip weed growth. The subsequent crop should suffer less weed infestation. What reasons can you give for this?

Densely planted beans

Plants vary in their climatic requirements. Tomatoes, cabbage and lettuce thrive well in the dry season, whereas yam, corn and cassava need large quantities of water in their early growing periods. They are generally planted in the months of May or June, that is, in the early weeks of the wet season. Most farmers rotate their crops to suit the seasonal conditions under which each crop grows best.

Crop rotation helps to stabilise farm labour and income. It enables farmer Kumar to grow crops throughout the year under varying seasonal and climatic conditions, so the farmer and his workers are always employed on the farm. There is a steady output of products and this helps to maintain regular incomes for the farmer and his employees.

Summary

Crop rotation is an agricultural practice in which a farmer does not grow the same crop on the same plot in succession, that is, all the time. By rotating crops the following advantages are gained.

1 Crop rotation helps to improve and maintain soil fertility and to make maximum and efficient use of soil nutrients. In this context three factors must be considered.

   a Crops vary in their nutrient requirements. Some plants need more of a particular type of nutrient and loss of others. By rotating crops efficient use is made of the available nutrients in the soil.

   b Some crops are deep rooted while others are shallow-rooted. Rotating a deep-rooted crop with a shallow-rooted crop facilitates the uptake of nutrients at varying levels in the soil.

   c Crops like corn and lettuce exhaust the soil of its nitrogen, while others, like legumes, add nitrogen. Rotating a legume with a soil-exhausting crop helps to maintain the balance of nitrogen in the soil.

2 Crop rotation is a means of controlling pests and diseases in crops. By rotating crops, pests and diseases do not get a chance to build up as different crops are likely to be attacked by different types of pests and diseases.

3 In a rotation the land has to be ploughed and prepared for each new crop. In the process, weeds are destroyed and turned into the soil to add to its organic content.

4 Crops could be rotated to suit the seasonal conditions under which they grow best.

5 Crop rotation facilitates the production of crops throughout the year under varying seasonal and climatic conditions. This helps to stabilise farm labour and income.

Remember these

Aeration	The movement of air in and out of the soil.
Crop rotation	An agricultural practice in which the same crop is not grown on the same plot in succession.
Drainage	Removal of excess water in the soil.
Foliage	The leafy parts of plants.
Nitrogen	An important nutrient element mainly responsible for shoot and leaf growth in plants.
Nutrients	Elements essential for the growth and development of plants.
Phosphate	An essential plant nutrient which promotes root and tuber development.
Planting distance	The distance between one plant and another within rows and between rows.
Toxic substances	Substances that are harmful to the roots of plants and to useful soil organisms.
Weed competition	The presence of weeds which compete with cultivated plants for light, water and nutrient supplies.

Practical activities

1 Examine the root system of the crops listed below and
then complete the table by classifying them as (a) surface
feeders and (b) deep feeders.

cabbage, sorrel, hot peppers, snap beans, patchoi, carrot,
melongene, pigeon peas, celery, ochro

Surface feeders	Deep feeders

Explain the importance of rotating crops that are surface
feeders with crops that are deep feeders.

2 Gently uproot a few four-to five-week old cow pea or
bodi bean plants and observe them for the presence of
root nodules. Make a sketch of the root system and label
the root nodules.

3 Study the crop rotation plan at the start of this chapter.
Make a similar plan of your own for the rotation of the

following crops: patchoi, melongene, sweet potatoes and black-eye bodi beans. Now use the plan and conduct a crop rotation programme in your home or school garden.

4 Select two plots of the same soil type in your home or school garden and label them plot A and plot B. On plot A grow two crops of lettuce in succession. On plot B grow a crop of bodi beans followed by a crop of lettuce. Do not use fertilisers.

Compare the growth of the second crop of lettuce on plot A with the crop of lettuce which followed the bodi beans on plot B. Comment on the state of growth and give reasons for differences you may have observed.

Do these test exercises

1 In parts a to d, select the best answer from the choices given.

a Which crop rotation programme should be recommended to a vegetable farmer?
A Tomato, lettuce, bodi bean, carrot.
B Carrot, lettuce, tomato, bodi bean.
C Bodi bean, tomato, lettuce, carrot.
D Carrot, tomato, bodi bean, lettuce.

b A crop which helps to enrich the soil with nitrogen is:
A tomato
B cow pea
C lettuce
D carrot

c Nitrogen is needed in large quantities by:
A vegetable fruit crops.
B vegetable root crops.
C leafy vegetable crops.
D leguminous crops.

d The best time to plant yam is in:
A February
B May
C August
D November

e Drainage is essential to:
(i) remove excess water from the soil.
(ii) improve soil aeration.
(iii) encourage the development of useful soil organisms.

In the statement above:
A only (i) is correct.
B Only (ii) is correct.
C (i), (ii) and (iii) are all correct.
D (i), (ii) and (iii) are all correct but (ii) and (iii) are dependent on (i).

2 Say why:
a Crops belonging to the same family group should not follow each other in a crop-rotating plan.
b A bean crop should be followed by a leaf crop in a rotation system.
c Corn is considered a soil exhausting crop.

d Pumpkins and cucumbers suffer from the same types of leaf disease.

3 Say how:
a Crop rotation helps to make better use of soil nutrients.
b Soil fertility is maintained when crops are rotated.
c Grasses in a crop rotation plan improve soil aeration and facilitate water movement in the soil.
d Close planting distances control weed growth.

4 Complete the paragraph below by incorporating the following ideas into it: grow crops throughout the year; under varying seasonal conditions; keeps farm workers regularly employed; maintains steady incomes.

Crop rotation enables a farmer to grow crops ....

5 Make a list of four crops that are (a) best grown in the dry season, (b) best suited for cultivation in the wet season and (c) could be grown successfully under both wet and dry conditions.

5

Water and nutrient requirements of garden plants

Lesson objectives

Plants grow and increase in size and weight as a result of the water and nutrient supplies that the roots absorb from the soil. On completing this lesson you should be able to:

1 explain how plants obtain water from the soil.

2 list the functions of water in plants.

3 describe how plants control their water supply.

4 explain how farmers ensure an optimum supply of soil water for their crops.

5 explain how plants obtain their nutrient supplies.

6 list the nutrients required by plants.

7 explain the functions of a few selected nutrients in plant growth and development.

8 list the agricultural practices adopted by farmers to maintain an adequate and balanced amount of available soil nutrients.

The picture at the top of page 53 shows you a seedling at transplanting time then at the third and then at the sixth week after transplanting. Observe the seedling at the three stages of growth. Compare the first stage with the second and third stages of growth and then find out the following.

Is there an increase in the number of leaves?

Is there an increase in size, that is, in height and stem thickness?

Will there be an increase in weight as well?

You will notice the increase in the number of leaves, the size of the plant and ultimately in the weight of the plant.

Do you know what is responsible for these increases? It is the nutrient and water supplies that the roots absorb from the soil. Let us try to find out how the plant does this.

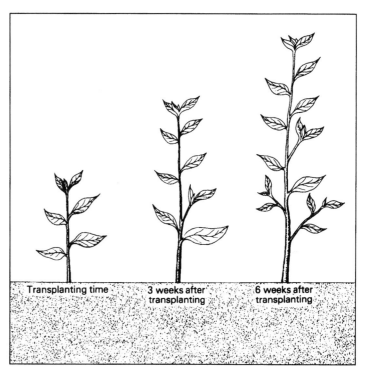

Transplanting time   3 weeks after transplanting   6 weeks after transplanting

The absorption and movement of water in plants

The plant gets its mineral and water requirements from the water in the soil together with the minerals dissolved in it. Water is taken up by the root hairs by the process of **osmosis** – that is, the movement of water through a semi-permeable membrane from a solution of a low concentration to that of a higher concentration.

The **cell sap** in the root hair is more concentrated than the soil solution. An osmotic pressure or suction is set up in the root and water from the soil solution passes through the cell wall, the semi-permeable cytoplasmic membrane and into the vacuole. When the vacuole is filled with water, the cell is said to be turgid.

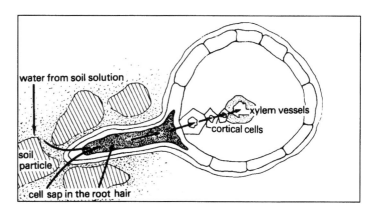

water from soil solution
xylem vessels
cortical cells
soil particle
cell sap in the root hair

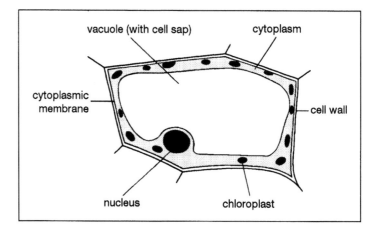

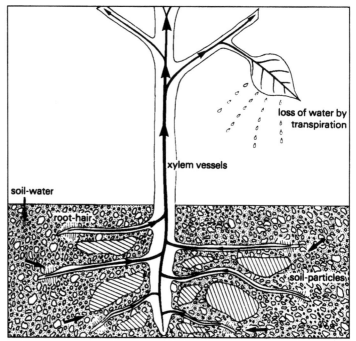

The water absorbed continues to move from cell to cell by means of osmosis and finally finds its way into the root xylem, which is a vessel that conducts water and other substances upward into the plant. From here the water moves through the xylem of the stem, the leaf petioles, the midrib and the leaf veins to the rest of the leaves and out to the atmosphere through little openings in the leaves called **stomata**. This loss of water to the atmosphere is known as **transpiration**. Once the process of transpiration begins, there is a continuous upward movement of water in the plant.

Why does a plant need water?

Water serves many useful functions in a plant. It maintains plant **turgidity** and it is essential in the process of photosynthesis and in the development of flowers and fruits. Water is also important in the germination of seeds.

In the presence of severe water shortages plant growth is retarded. The plant may also wilt and die.

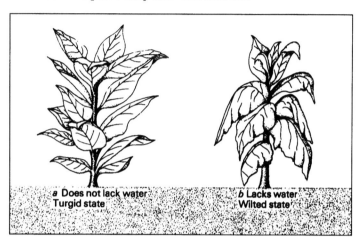

a Does not lack water
Turgid state

b Lacks water
Wilted state

How the plant controls its water loss

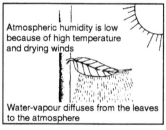

Atmospheric humidity is low because of high temperature and drying winds

Water-vapour diffuses from the leaves to the atmosphere

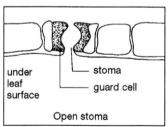

under leaf surface — stoma
— guard cell

Open stoma

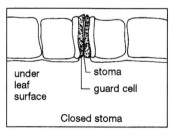

under leaf surface — stoma
— guard cell

Closed stoma

We have learned that water is lost from the leaves of a plant during transpiration. This usually takes place in the presence of high temperatures or drying winds, when the humidity in the atmosphere is low. Water vapour diffuses out of the stomatal openings into the surrounding atmosphere.

The plant controls its water supply by the actions of the **guard cells** which open or close the stomatal aperture. When the guard cells are turgid, that is, filled with water, the stoma opens. When they are flaccid (that is, short of water) the stoma closes.

Sometimes the plant shows temporary wilting. This happens when the rate of water lost from the plant during transpiration is greater than the rate of water absorbed by the roots of the plants.

Temporary wilting

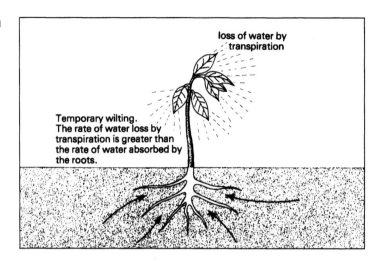

Temporary wilting.
The rate of water loss by
transpiration is greater than
the rate of water absorbed by
the roots.

loss of water by
transpiration

How the farmer controls the water requirements of his crops

Crops need an optimum supply of soil water, that is, water available in the soil for plant use. There must be neither too much nor too little water in the soil.

Farmers use several methods to control and ensure an optimum supply of soil water for their crops. The methods used depend on the kind of crop grown, the soil type, and the season of the year in which the crop is cultivated.

Lagoon rice (left) is grown in swampy areas or in small plots that are bunded around and irrigated. Watercress (below left) grows best in places through which cool fresh water flows.

On sandy soils farmers construct shallow drains. Very often drains are not needed at all. In such soils the addition of pen manure and other organic substances helps to retain water and increase the growth and yields of crops. This is known as mulching. Heavy clays must be well tilled and deeply drained. Crops grown on clays thrive best on raised plots and ridges.

Under very wet conditions, the soil must be thoroughly drained before planting. In the dry season irrigation and mulching are often needed to maintain and conserve soil water for garden crops.

The diagram on page 57 shows you two types of irrigation system. Which of these is best suited to your school garden?

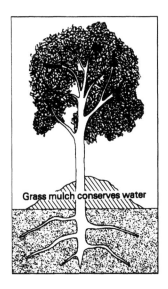

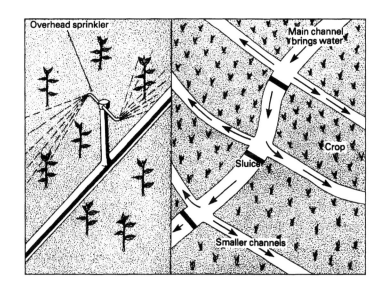

Observe the grass mulch used on the surface of the soil to prevent evaporation of soil water. In this way water is conserved in the soil for plant use.

How plants absorb nutrients

You will remember that the nutrient and water supplies absorbed by the roots of plants were largely responsible for the plant's increase in size and weight as it grew older. You will remember, too, that water is absorbed by the root hairs in the process of osmosis.

How does the plant get and utilise its nutrient supplies?

Plants obtain most of their nutrient supply from the soil. Small quantities of mineral salts diffuse into the cells of the root as they come into contact with the soil solution. Young roots have the ability to accumulate free 'ions' from the soil solution. Ions are electrically charged chemical particles. By this means plants build up salt concentrations in their cells.

The process of accumulating salts takes place in the presence of oxygen. As a result, we must keep our garden soils well aerated by means of tillage and drainage.

The nutrient requirements of plants

Garden plants require many nutrients. Carbon and oxygen are obtained from the atmosphere during the process of photosynthesis. Hydrogen is derived directly or indirectly from the soil water. All other nutrients are obtained from the soil.

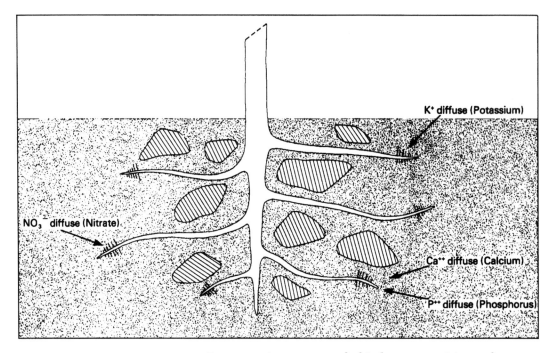

Some nutrients are needed in large quantities and are termed **macro-nutrients**. These are nitrogen, phosphorus, potassium, calcium, magnesium, and sulphur. The growth and yield of crops may be retarded if these nutrients are lacking in the soil or if they are in short supply. The wrong balance (imbalance) of these nutrients may also affect our crops.

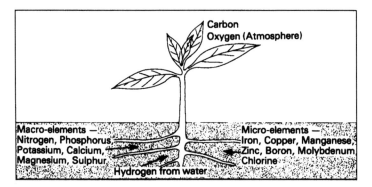

Some other nutrients are used in very small amounts by our crops. These are called **micro-nutrients**. They are iron, copper, manganese, zinc, boron, molybdenum, and chlorine. The absence of these micro-nutrients may lead to deficiency diseases. In excess, they may be poisonous to the plant.

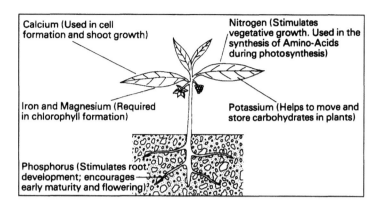

Study this diagram and observe the role played by some of the nutrients in the growth and development of crops:

The farmer ploughs and drains the soil. These operations remove excess soil water, improve aeration, and increase root room. Under dry conditions irrigation is necessary to maintain water supply and the availability of nutrients.

Lime can be added to the soil. This helps to remove soil acidity and increases the solubility of iron and phosphates.

The farmer makes full use of manures and fertilisers. These increase and replenish the nutrient supplies of the soil. Micro-nutrients are often applied to plants as **foliar sprays**, that is, the elements are mixed in solution and sprayed on the foliage of the plants.

Crop rotation maintains and increases soil fertility. Leafy crops like lettuce, patchoi, and cabbage tend to deplete the soil of nitrogen, whereas crops like peas and beans help to increase the nitrogen content of the soil.

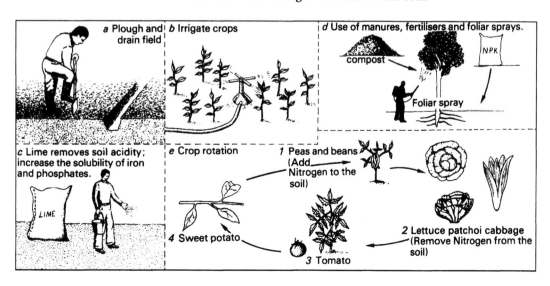

Summary

The plant obtains its mineral and water requirements from soil water with the minerals dissolved in it. Water is taken up by the root hairs in the process of osmosis. The water absorbed moves from cell to cell until it enters the xylem vessels and then moves upwards through the stem, the leaf petioles, the midrib, the leaf veins and to the rest of the leaves. Excess water from the leaf is lost to the atmosphere through transpiration.

Water serves many useful functions in a plant. It maintains plant turgidity, and it is needed in the process of photosynthesis and in the development of flowers and fruits. Water is also important in the germination of seeds. In times of water shortage, plant growth is retarded. The plant may also wilt and die.

The plant controls its water supply by the action of the guard cells which open or close the stomatal apertures. These generally lie in the under surface of the leaf. Under very dry conditions it is often necessary to irrigate crops and practise mulching.

Plants obtain most of their nutrient supplies from the soil. Small quantities of mineral salts diffuse into the cells of the roots as they come into contact with the soil solution. Young roots accumulate free ions from the soil solution and build up concentrations of salt in their cells.

Plants require many nutrients. They obtain carbon and oxygen from the air and hydrogen from soil water. Some nutrients such as nitrogen, phosphorus, potassium, calcium, magnesium and sulphur are needed in large quantities and these are termed macro-nutrients. Other nutrients such as iron, copper, manganese, zinc, boron, molybdenum and chlorine are needed in very small amounts and are known as micro-nutrients. Shortages of macro- or micro-nutrients affect crop yields and cause deficiency diseases.

Garden crops grow well in the presence of adequate and balanced amounts of available soil nutrients. These amounts can be ensured by proper drainage, good soil aeration and the maintenance of soil water and available plant nutrients.

The use of lime, manures, fertilisers, foliar sprays and the practice of crop rotation help to ensure that crops get the nutrients they require.

Remember these

Cell sap	The presence of water with dissolved mineral salts in the vacuole of the cell.
Foliar spray	A fertiliser solution applied as a spray to foliage.
Guard cells	Cells which control the opening and closing of the stoma in a leaf.
Macro-nutrients	Nutrients needed in large quantities by plants.
Micro-nutrients	Nutrients required in small amounts by plants.
Osmosis	The movement of water through a semi-permeable membrane from a solution of low concentration to that of a higher concentration.
Stomata	Small openings or pores generally present in the under surface of the leaf (the singular is *stoma*).
Transpiration	The loss of excess water from the leaf to the atmosphere through the stomatal openings.
Turgidity	The state or condition of the plant when high levels of cell sap are present in the plant tissue.
Xylem vessels	Conducting vessels in a plant which carry water and dissolved mineral salts from the roots to other parts of the plant.

Practical activities

1 Collect fifty tomato seedlings of the same size, health, and vigour, and transplant them in your garden plot. Make the following observations at the time of transplanting, and again at the third and at the sixth week after planting. Examine ten seedlings in each case.

	Observations				
	Number of plants examined	Average number of leaves	Average height from roots to terminal bud	Average circumference of stem 10 cm above ground	Average weight of plant
1 At transplanting time	10				
2 At third week	10				
3 At sixth week	10				

Look at your results at the end of the sixth week, and compare them with those at the time of transplanting.

Was there an increase in the number of leaves?

Did the plants increase in height and stem thickness?

Did the plants increase in weight?

You will have noticed that the plants increased both in size and in weight. Explain what was responsible for this.

2 Try this experiment.

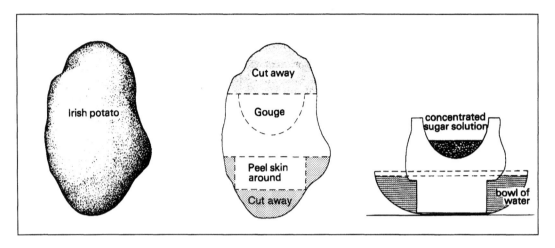

Take an Irish potato and cut transverse sections at the top and bottom. Gouge a hole at the top end of the potato and fill with concentrated sugar solution to a marked height. Rest the potato to half its height in a bowl of water and observe it ten hours later. What do you notice about the level of the sugar solution in the potato? Give an explanation for your observation.

3 Take a potted plant that is in a high state of turgor and place it in a spot where it will not get moisture from natural rainfall. Avoid watering the plant so that it will reach the stage of wilting. Now water the plant heavily and leave overnight. Make your observations on the next day and give an explanation for any differences observed.

4 Select two shrubs e.g. crotons in your school compound and mulch one of them with dry grass to a thickness of 10 cm covering the surface of the soil from the stem of the plant to a distance of 60 cm around. Do this in the first week of January. Do not irrigate the plants. Make observations on both plants after a 6 to 8 week dry spell. Give explanations for any differences observed.

5 Prepare two clay pots with a sandy loam that is identical. Place a lettuce plant in each pot (both plants must be of the same stage of growth and state of vigour) and label the pots A and B respectively. Irrigate both pots with plain water once every other day. To pot B alone apply 200 ml of a nitrogen solution (1 teaspoonful of urea to 4 litres of water) once per week. Make observations on both potted plants after 4 weeks.

a Give explanations for any differences observed.

b In what way can the farmer use the information obtained in this experiment to improve his crops?

1 Consider these statements carefully. State whether they are *true* or *false*.

a Plants obtain all their nutrient supplies from the soil.

b Mineral absorption is greater in well aerated soil.

c Tanspiration assists the upward movement of water in plants.

d Micro nutrients are required by plants in large quantities.

e Cell sap is composed of water and dissolved mineral substances.

2 Select the best answer from the choices given.

a The root hair takes up water from the soil by the process of:

A suction

B diffusion

C osmosis

D transpiration

b Transpiration usually takes place in the presence of:

A high temperatures

B drying winds

C low humidity

D all of the above

c The guard cells are associated with the:

A root hairs

B stomatal pores

C leaf petioles

D cell vacuoles

d An example of a macro-nutrient is:

A boron

B manganese

C potassium

D copper

e Mulching is practised mainly to:

A conserve soil water

B control weed growth

C increase soil organic content

D maintain soil fertility

3 Say why:

a temporary wilting takes place in plants.

b irrigation is necessary in the dry season.

c deep drains are not necessary in sandy soils.

4 Explain how:

a Drainage improves aeration.

b Mulching conserves soil water.

c Plants control their water supply.

d Plants absorb nutrients from the soil.

5 Say how a farmer ensures an optimum supply of water for his crops under the following conditions:

a On sandy soils.

b On clayey soils.

c In the dry season.

d In the wet season.

e On low-lying lands.

6 Prepare a list of:

a Macro-nutrients needed by plants.

b Micro-nutrients needed by plants.

7 Describe the process of osmosis.

8 List and explain the agricultural practices that a farmer can adopt to maintain an adequate and balanced amount of available soil nutrients for his crops.

9 Explain the role played by the following nutrients in the growth and development of crops: Nitrogen, phosphorus, potassium, calcium, magnesium and iron.

6

Manures and fertilisers I

Lesson objectives

Manures and fertilisers are organic or inorganic in nature. In this lesson the emphasis is on organic manures. On completing the lesson you should be able to:

1 define the nutrient cycle.

2 describe how the nutrient cycle works.

3 differentiate between the terms 'organic manures' and 'inorganic manures'.

4 list sources of organic manures.

5 give simple descriptions of different types of organic manures.

6 describe the process of compost making.

7 explain how protein compounds are broken down to form nitrates.

8 explain the importance of the carbon and nitrogen cycles in nature.

9 state the importance of organic manures in the soil.

Plants need adequate amounts of water and mineral supplies for healthy growth and good crop yields. Minerals present in the soil solution are generally derived from the organic content of the soil, the decomposition of rocks and minerals, from the application of manures and fertilisers.

Manures and fertilisers exist in a variety of forms. Let us find out more about them and how they are used in agricultural production.

The nutrient cycle

In your village or district you may see the wild growth of bushes and forest trees. Nature ensures the nutrient supplies of these plants in a process that is known as the

In nature vegetation is sustained by means of the nutrient cycle. Plant nutrients are derived from the organic and inorganic substances present in the soil.

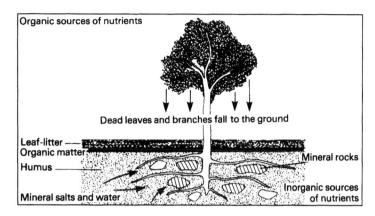

Organic sources of nutrients

Dead leaves and branches fall to the ground

Leaf-litter
Organic matter
Humus
Mineral rocks
Inorganic sources of nutrients
Mineral salts and water

nutrient cycle. This diagram shows how this operates.

Mineral rocks are broken down in the process of weathering to release **inorganic** mineral salts. These salts are dissolved in the soil water to form soil solutions, which are absorbed by the roots of the plants.

Dead leaves, branches, and roots, as well as the droppings and dead bodies of animals, fall to the ground. These 'organic' substances are decomposed and mineralised by the activities of soil micro-organisms under moist conditions, to form 'humus'. This is the organic source of our plant nutrient supplies.

A tree crop like cocoa generally obtains its nutrient requirements by means of the nutrient cycle. Crops like cabbages and tomatoes cannot depend on this cycle completely. They must be given fertilisers regularly.

Sources of manures and fertilisers

Do you know what a manure or fertiliser is? It is any substance or substances which, when added to the soil, help to increase and improve the soils fertility.

Farmer applying pen manure to the soil on which cabbage is grown.

Pen manure

Cabbage

Some manures are organic. Others, like nitrate of soda or sulphate of ammonia are 'inorganic'. These are obtained from minerals or manufactured synthetically.

A factory where chemical fertilisers are manufactured and prepared for use by farmers.

Organic manures

The several types of organic manure are (a) pen or farmyard manures, (b) compost manures, (c) liquid manures, (d) green manures, (e) other organic manures.

Pen or farmyard manures

These are obtained from stables and livestock pens. They consist of litter or straw, and the solid and liquid excrements of the animals. Farmyard manure is best tilled into the soil when it is fully rotted. In its raw state, it may burn the plants.

A healthy plant (left) and one burnt by manures (right)

In the early stages of decomposition there is high micro-bial activity, accompanied by heat. The microbes may also extract soil nitrogen to build up their own bodies, so the plants may suffer a temporary lack of nitrogen.

Compost manures

On a mixed farm there may be large quantities of plant and animal waste. These materials are composted, that is, put together in a heap and allowed to decompose to form valu-able manures for our garden crops. In a later section we will look at compost-making in greater detail.

Liquid manures

The liquids collected from the washings of pens are known as **liquid manures**. These consist of animal urine and small amounts of solid droppings dissolved in water.

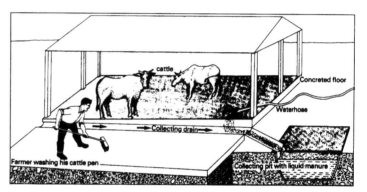

Liquid manures are very rich in nitrogen, because urine contains urea, a substance that contains a lot of nitrogen. Liquid manures in their concentrated state are very harm-ful to plants. They must be diluted before use. Why?

Green manures

Mr Habib is enriching his plot by rotavating a legume crop into it.

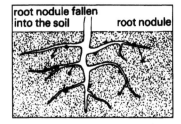

root nodule fallen into the soil

root nodule

How does a legume crop enrich the soil? You will remember that legumes are able to extract nitrogen from the atmosphere and store some of it in tiny root nodules. This is done in the presence of certain soil bacteria. The nodules fall and decompose in the soil. The bacteria die and leave behind large quantities of nitrogen in the soil. On the other hand, the green parts of the plant decompose to increase the organic content of the soil.

Several leguminous crops can be used as **green manures**. the ones in common use are cow peas, black-eye bodi-beans, urdi or woolly pyrol and *Crotalaria*.

Now can you tell why Mr Habib always plants a leaf crop in his garden plot after harvesting a bean crop?

Other organic manures

There are many other organic materials that have value as manure. They may or may not be used in your country. **Guano**, that is the droppings of wild birds, the remains of meat and fish industries and the sludge from sewers are all processed and sold as fertilisers. The residues of plant industries, such as coffee and cocoa husks, sawdust, citrus pulp, and filter-press mud from the sugar-mills are all incorporated into the soil as manures.

The garden compost heap

A compost heap can be described as a spot or structure located in the farm where plant and animal remains are put to decompose to form manure. Study the diagram on this page and try to find out more about garden compost. Why are bottles, stones and so on not desirable?

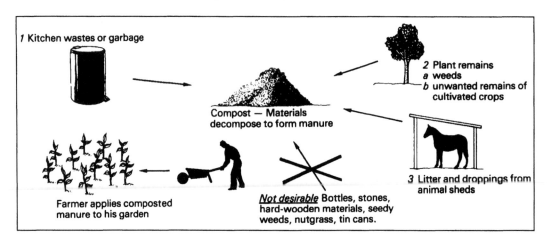

1 Kitchen wastes or garbage

2 Plant remains
a weeds
b unwanted remains of cultivated crops

Compost — Materials decompose to form manure

3 Litter and droppings from animal sheds

Farmer applies composted manure to his garden

Not desirable Bottles, stones, hard-wooden materials, seedy weeds, nutgrass, tin cans.

Compost

Siting the compost heap

The compost heap should be sited at a convenient spot, within easy reach of available composting materials and as near as possible to the garden site where the manure is to be used. A well-drained site, under a cool shady tree, is ideal. Exposure to heavy rains or direct sunlight results in the loss of plant nutrients by **leaching** or evaporation.

Making the compost

Farmer Dass gathers composting materials well in advance and makes compost in three phases.

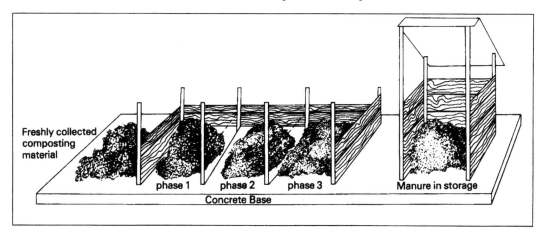

Freshly collected composting material

phase 1   phase 2   phase 3   Manure in storage

Concrete Base

Phase 1

At the bottom of the compost a 10 cm layer of pen manure or rotted compost is placed as a starter. In this way Farmer Dass introduces the desirable micro-organisms into the compost. On this first layer he places a 25 cm layer of damp composting material. He then incorporates about 1.5 kg of sulphate of ammonia and about 500 g of ground limestone. These provide the necessary conditions for microbial activity, and the quick breakdown of the compost.

The compost is built up by the addition of alternate layers of starter and composting materials as described above. The process continues until a height of 1.5 or 2 m is reached.

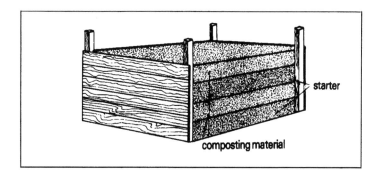

starter

composting material

Farmer Dass ensures that the compost is not tightly stacked, as this hinders aeration and decomposition. This phase extends over a period of three to four weeks.

Phase 2
The composted material from phase 1 is turned into phase 2. All undecomposed materials should be placed at the bottom of the new heap. Turning assists in the quick and even decomposition of the heap. This phase lasts for another three to four weeks.

Phase 3
Phase 3 completes the process of decomposition. At the end of the second or third week the compost is used in the garden or stacked under cover for future use.

The process of composting is a continuous one. Composting materials should be collected regularly and phased in so there will be a regular supply of manure.

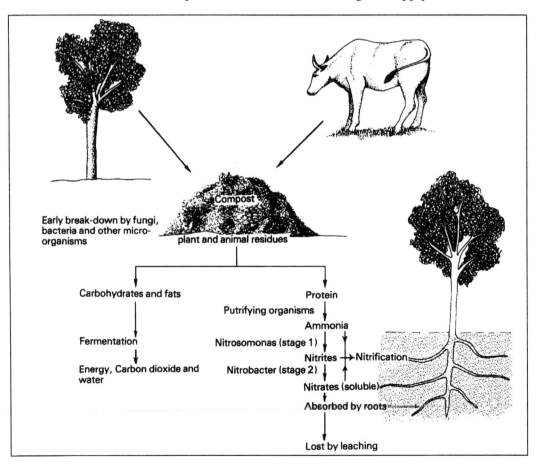

How the compost is decomposed to form manures

Observe a handful of garden compost carefully. You will notice that it is dark in colour and quite different from the original materials composted.

The diagram on page 70 will help you to understand how the compost is decomposed to form manures for plant use.

In the process of decomposition, plant and animal residues are broken down by fungi, bacteria and other micro-organisms into carbohydrates, fats and protein compounds. The carbohydrates and fats undergo fermentation to produce energy, carbon dioxide and water. The protein compounds are acted upon by putrifying organisms to produce ammonia. This compound is further broken down by the nitrifying bacteria *nitrosomonas* and *nitrobacter* to produce nitrites and nitrates. Nitrates are soluble and are readily absorbed by the roots of plants or lost from the soil in the process of leaching.

You need to know that the decomposition process is closely associated with the **carbon and nitrogen cycles** which operate in nature. The former helps to maintain the balance of carbon and oxygen in the atmosphere and the latter relates mainly to the removal and addition of nitrogen in the soil.

Study these cycles and try to understand them.

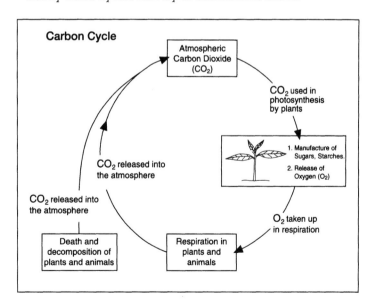

Carbon Cycle

Atmospheric Carbon Dioxide (CO_2)

CO_2 used in photosynthesis by plants

1. Manufacture of Sugars, Starches.
2. Release of Oxygen (O_2)

CO_2 released into the atmosphere

CO_2 released into the atmosphere

Death and decomposition of plants and animals

Respiration in plants and animals

O_2 taken up in respiration

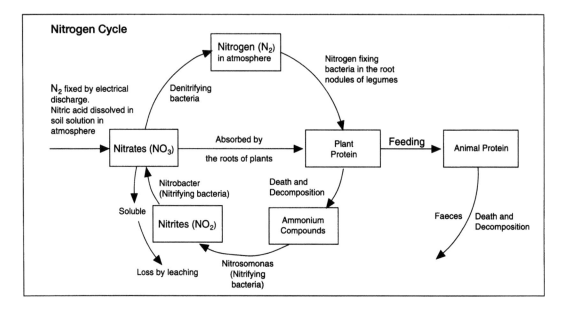

The role of organic matter in the soil

In Book One we learned that organic matter binds sand and separates clays. The effect of this binding and separating assists in the formation of soil granules or aggregates. The soil becomes porous, better drained, and better aerated.

Many useful soil micro-organisms feed and thrive on organic matter. These microbes break down complex organic substances and mineralise them for plant use.

Organic manures improve the soil physically. They are rich in plant nutrients and have the ability to absorb and retain water in the soil.

Summary

Plants obtain their nutrient supplies from the organic content of the soil, the decomposition of mineral rocks and from the application of manures and fertilisers.

In nature vegetation is sustained by means of the 'nutrient cycle', a process in which organic substances are decomposed, mineralised and re-absorbed by the roots of plants.

Manures and fertilisers are classified as organic, that is, derived from plant and animal origin or inorganic, that is, obtained from mineral rocks or manufactured synthetically. In this lesson the emphasis is on organic manures.

There are several types of organic manures. Some of these are pen or farmyard manures, compost manures, liquid manures, green manures and several other organic substances used as manures.

Pen or farmyard manures are obtained from horse stables and pens of cows, pigs, goats and poultry. These manures consist of litter and the solid and liquid excrement of animals. Pen manure must be properly rotted before it is applied to crops.

Compost manures are derived from plant and animal waste which undergo decomposition and mineralisation in a practice known as composting. The nitrogen cycle and the carbon cycle, which maintain the balance of carbon dioxide and oxygen in the atmosphere, are associated with the nitrification process in compost production.

Liquid manures are liquids collected from the washing of pens. This consists of urine and small amounts of solids dissolved in water. Liquid manures are very rich in nitrogen and must be diluted before use.

Green manuring is the process of ploughing a legume crop into the soil. The root nodules decompose and leave large quantities of nitrogen in the soil whilst the green parts of the plant increase the organic content of the soil.

Many other organic substances are used as manures. These include guano and the processed remains of the meat and fish industries, the sludge from sewers and residues of plant industries (such as coffee and cocoa husk), sawdust, citrus pulp and filter press mud.

Organic manure is important in the soil as follows:

1 It separates clays and bind sands. This improves soil structure, making the soil porous, better drained and better aerated.

2 It provides organic matter for the development and activities of useful soil organisms. These organisms decompose and mineralise organic substances for plant use.

3 Organic matter is a rich source of plant nutrients. It absorbs and retains water in the soil.

Remember these

Carbon cycle   A cycle in nature mainly responsible for the balance of carbon dioxide and oxygen in the atmosphere.

Compost manure   Manures produced by composting crop and animal residues available on a farm.

Green manures	Leguminous crops used in improving soil fertility.
Guano	Manures derived from the droppings of wild birds.
Inorganic compounds	Substances obtained from the break-down of mineral or manufactured synthetically.
Leaching	The movements of soluble nutrients down into the soil as a result of the infiltration of soil water.
Liquid manure	Material derived from the washing of pens, consisting mainly of urine and dissolved solid droppings.
Nitrogen cycle	A cycle in nature relating to the balance of nitrogen in the atmosphere.
Nutrient cycle	The sustenance of vegetation in nature by recycling nutrients derived from the decomposition and mineralisation of dead leaves, branches, roots and animal remains.
Organic manures	Manures derived from plant and animal residues.

Practical activities

1 Grow some corn seeds in (a) river sand, (b) good potting soil. Water the plants regularly and observe them until the end of the third week. What differences do you notice in growth? On which medium was better plant growth obtained? What reasons can you give for the differences in growth? What can you do to improve the plants growth on the poorer soil type? What does a farmer do to ensure that his field crops get an adequate supply of nutrients?

2 Set up a compost heap in your school farm. Collect composting materials and run the three-phase composting process like the one described in this lesson.

   a How is the compost manure different from the original materials that were composted?

   b Explain how protein compounds are broken down to form nitrates.

3 Select two plots in your school garden of the same soil type, well ploughed and properly drained. Label the plots A and B. Plant both with patchoi seedlings that are the same age, size and state of health.

   Keep both plots free from weeds and irrigate regularly. Apply dilute liquid manure to Plot B only, once a week. Make your observations at the end of the fourth week after planting. Give explanations for any differences.

4 Grow a crop of cow peas or bodi-beans and turn it into the soil at the flowering stage.

   a What is this method of soil improvement called?

   b Explain how the soil is enriched in this process.

5 Collect and label samples of the following:

a Organic manures, for example pen manure, compost manure, liquid manure.

b Residues from plant industries for example coffee and cocoa husk, saw dust, citrus pulp, filter press mud.

c Seeds of legumes used as green manures, for example cow peas, bodi beans, woolly pyrol, *crotalaria*.

Place these samples in your school laboratory.

1 Consider these statements carefully. State whether they are true or false.

a Inorganic fertilisers are derived from mineral rocks.

b It is a desirable practice to follow a leaf crop with a bean crop.

c In the process of respiration carbon dioxide is taken in and oxygen released.

d Organic manures improve the water holding capacity of sandy soil.

e Nitrates are derived from protein compounds.

2 Select the best answers from the choices given.

a Which crop is best suited for use in a green manuring programme.

A celery

B bodi beans

C carrots

D Tomatoes

b A farmer collected the washing from his cattle pen and diluted it for use as a fertiliser to his cabbage crop. This type of fertiliser is described as

A pen manure

B green manure

C compost manure

D liquid manure

c In the nitrogen cycle *nitrobacters* are responsible for the

A fixation of nitrogen in the root nodules of legumes.

B nitrification of ammonium compounds into nitrites.

C nitrification of nitrites into nitrates.

D denitrification of nitrates into nitrogen.

d Which of the following is considered undesirable as compost material.

A seedy weeds

B kitchen waste

C crop residues

D animal droppings

e The carbon cycle relates to the atmospheric balance of

A carbon dioxide and nitrogen.

B carbon dioxide and oxygen.

C oxygen and nitrogen.

D oxygen and hydrogen.

3 List four sources of organic manures. Give a simple description of any two of the sources listed.

4 Describe how the addition of organic manures can increase the water-holding capacity of sandy soils.

5 What is the most economical way to enrich the soil for a cabbage crop?

6 Say why:

a crops are fertilised.

b dilute liquid manures are good for leaf-crops.

c well rotted manures must be protected from the weather, that is, the rain and the sun.

d Ground limestone and sulphate of ammonia are incorporated into a compost.

e Top or surface soil is dark in colour.

7 Say how:

a plant nutrients are released from mineral rocks.

b legume crops enrich the soil.

c aeration is improved in clayey soil with the addition of pen manure.

d protein compounds of plant and animal residues are converted in the soil to nitrates.

8 In each case give four examples of:

a organic manures derived from plant industries.

b legumes that are grown and used as green manures.

c materials that should not be included in the compost.

7 Manures and fertilisers II

Lesson objectives

Large quantities of inorganic fertilisers are generally used in an intensive cropping system. These fertilisers affect plant growth and development in several ways and should be applied with great care. On completing this lesson you should be able to:

1 define the term 'inorganic fertilisers'.

2 list sources of inorganic fertilisers.

3 give simple descriptions of inorganic fertilisers.

4 state the effect of fertilisers on plant growth and development.

5 describe the methods of fertiliser placement in the soil.

6 explain how the application of fertilisers in very strong concentration affect plants.

Inorganic fertilisers

Farmer Dass does intensive cropping. This means that his land is always cultivated. He fertilises his crops with large quantities of inorganic or chemical manures usually known as inorganic fertilisers. You will remember that inorganic fertilisers are obtained from mineral rocks or manufactured synthetically.

The three major elements required for plant growth are nitrogen (N) phosphorus (P) and potassium (K). These chemicals are absorbed in solution by the roots of plants as **nitrates**, phosphates, and salts of potash. Inorganic manures containing these chemicals are sold as **simple fertilisers**, mainly for one element or as complete or mixed fertilisers. **Complete fertilisers** consist of mixtures of nitrogen, phosphorus and potassium in different proportions or ratios. These ratios are written on the labels of the sacks containing the fertiliser.

Simple fertilisers may be grouped as follows: (a) nitrogenous (N), (b) phosphatic (P), (c) potash (K). In each group are fertilisers of different combinations and strengths.

Nitrogenous fertilisers

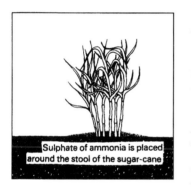

Sulphate of ammonia is placed around the stool of the sugar-cane

Sulphate of ammonia (20.6 per cent N)
This is a white crystalline substance. It absorbs very little moisture from the atmosphere, and dissolves very readily in water. Sulphate of ammonia is not very expensive, and is used extensively in plantations and vegetable gardens.

Ammonium nitrate (23–35 per cent N)
This varies in strength from 23 per cent to 35 per cent. It absorbs moisture from the atmosphere, and it is explosive in nature. In order to improve its handling and storage qualities it is pelleted and suitably coated.

Calcium nitrate, also called Cal-nitro (15–20 per cent N)
Calcium nitrate is a mixture of lime and ammonium nitrate. It is safe, easy to handle, and stores well. It reduces soil acidity that is left behind when nitrogen is removed from the soil.

Urea (46.6 per cent N)
Urea has a high nitrogen content. It decomposes in the soil to form ammonia. This is acted upon by bacteria, to form nitrates.

Urea is now used in small quantities as a source of nitrogen for the feeds of ruminant animals, that is, animals which eat grass and chew the cud.

Anhydrous ammonia gas (12 per cent N)
Liquefied ammonia gas is the cheapest form of nitrogenous fertiliser. It is injected into the soil where it dissolves in the **soil solution**. This fertiliser is not yet much used by farmers in the Caribbean.

You will remember that phosphates stimulate root development and assist in the early flowering and fruiting of crops. The most widely used phosphatic fertiliser is superphosphate. There are three grades of superphosphate.
a. Single superphosphate (16–21 per cent available phosphoric acid)
b. Double superphosphate (30–31 per cent available phosphoric acid)
c. Triple superphosphate (40–47 per cent available phosphoric acid)
Of the three grades, triple superphosphate is used most extensively. Other known phosphatic fertilisers in use are bonemeal, basic slag (a by-product of the iron-smelting industry) and ammonium phosphate.

Phosphates are readily fixed in the soil, that is, they combine with other elements in the soil to form **insoluble compounds**. These compounds are unavailable to the plant. Phosphate fixation could be reduced by the application of pen or compost manures to the garden plot.

Potash is needed especially at flowering and fruiting time

Potash
Earlier in this book we learnt that potassium helps to remove and store carbohydrates in plants. Potash is needed, especially at the time of flowering and fruit set.

Potassic fertilisers are analysed and rated on the percentage of potassium oxide they contain. The two most popular potassic fertilisers are:
(a) Muriate of potash (60 per cent potassium oxide)
(b) Sulphate of potash (48–50 per cent potassium oxide)
We must remember, too, that small quantities of potash are obtained in woodash.

Potash is not readily leached from loamy or clayey soils. However, many plants tend to absorb more potash than they actually need.

Complete or mixed
fertilisers

N.P.K. 5.10.5
N.P.K. 22.11.11
N.P.K. 10.10.10
N.P.K. 13.13.21

This list shows you different types of mixed fertilisers or complete fertilisers.

Name the chief elements that make up a mixed fertiliser.

Look at each fertiliser and state the ratios in which the elements are present.

Which fertiliser has the highest nitrogen content?

Which fertiliser is specially high in potash?

Which fertiliser has an equal balance of nitrogen, phosphorus and potassium?

Which mixed fertiliser has an additional trace element?

Give two advantages that mixed fertilisers have over simple fertilisers.

Complete or mixed fertilisers contain the chief elements nitrogen, phosphorus and potassium in definite proportions or ratios. Fertilisers with high nitrogen content are best suited for leaf crops or plants in their early **vegetative** stages of growth. Phosphates are essential for root development, whilst bearing crops require fertilisers with high quantities of potash.

Sometimes a nutrient element may be present in the soil in excess, or it may be in short supply. When this occurs there is an upset in the uptake of other elements, causing an imbalance in the nutrition of the plant.

Mixed fertilisers are now very popular. By their use, farmers apply the three major elements to their crops at the same time. They save time and labour and help to maintain the balance of plant nutrients in the soil.

Find out which fertiliser is best suited for (a) leaf crops, (b) plants in their vegetative stage of growth, (c) plants that are bearing, (d) root crops and root development, (e) lawns and pastures (f) general purposes.

It must be remembered that commercial fertilisers are also sold by other brand names in the garden shops. You should read their labels carefully before you buy them or apply them to your crops.

The application and placement of fertilisers

Farmer Dass applies fertilisers to his crops with great care. The type of fertiliser he applies depends upon the crop he grows and its stages of growth, the **available soil nutrients**, and the weather conditions.

Performing soil analysis

From a soil analysis the farmer finds out which elements are lacking in the soil. He supplies these by means of fertilisers. Farmer Dass also knows that the nutrient requirements of crops vary. As a result, he applies the type of fertilisers that are best suited to his crops.

The weather must be taken into consideration when fertilisers are to be applied. Some fertilisers, like nitrates, are soluble and are readily leached out of the soil. Under wet conditions such fertilisers should be applied in small quantities at closer intervals or periods of time.

Now, let us consider some of the ways in which fertilisers are placed in the soil or applied to crops.

Broadcasting

The fertilisers are **broadcast** on the surface of the ground and then soaked into the soil. This method is most suitable for lawns, pastures and field crops, such as rice or paddy.

Band application

Bands of fertiliser are placed along row crops or under orchard trees at the points where the leaves drip.

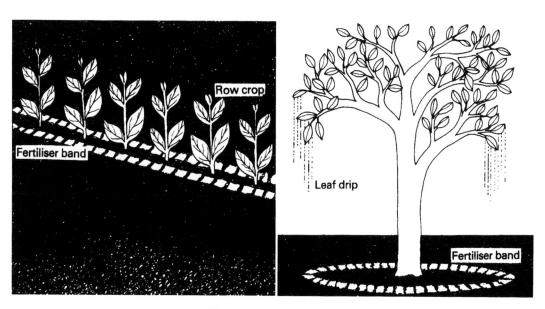

Drills

The fertiliser is drilled into the soil near the roots of the plants. Where mechanical planting is done the fertiliser may be drilled into the soil at planting time. How is this method of operation – that is, mechanical planting and fertilising at the same time – beneficial to the farmer and his crops?

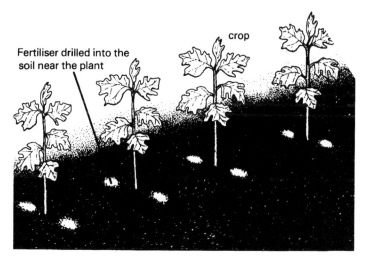

Liquid application

Solutions of fertilisers are made by diluting them with water. The solution is applied at intervals to the soil near the roots of the plants. It is important that the solution does not get on the stems or leaves of the plants, as this may cause scorching.

Foliar sprays

By this method the fertiliser is applied in solution as a spray to the leaves of the plant. This method is often used for the application of trace elements. Remember that plants require trace elements in very minute quantities, and these are absorbed by the foliage of the plants.

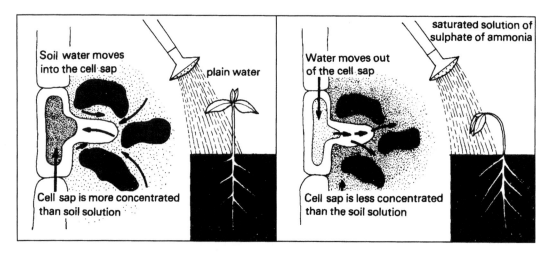

How heavy fertiliser application affects crops

Heavy applications of fertilisers make the soil solution around the roots of plants more concentrated than the solution in the cell sap of the root cells. As a result, water from the cell sap diffuses out of the root cells into the soil solution. The plant becomes dehydrated or **plasmolysed**. It finally collapses and dies. Fertilisers should never be applied in stronger doses than the strengths recommended.

Summary

Inorganic fertilisers generally cater for the three major plant nutrients which are nitrogen (N), phosphorus (P) and potassium (K). These fertilisers are sold as simple fertilisers, that is, for one element only, or as complete or mixed fertiliser, that is, mixtures of nitrogen, phosphorus and potassium in different ratios.

Simple fertilisers are classified as follows:

(a) Nitrogenous – Sulphate of ammonia (20.6% N)
   Ammonium nitrate (23–35% N)
   Calcium nitrate (15–20% N)
   Urea (46.6% N)
   Anhydrous ammonia gas (12% N)

(b) Phosphatic – Single superphosphate (16–21% available phosphoric acid)
   Double superphosphate (30–31% available phosphoric acid)
   Triple superphosphate (40–47% available phosphoric acid)
   Bone meal, basic slag

(c) Potash – Muriate of Potash – (60% potassium oxide)
   Sulphate of Potash – (48–50% potassium oxide)

Complete or mixed fertilisers contain the chief elements, nitrogen, phosphorus and potassium in definite proportions. Some of them may also contain trace elements, that is, elements plants need in very minute quantities.

The type of fertiliser applied depends upon the crop grown, the stage of growth, available soil nutrients and weather conditions.

Fertilisers are applied in several ways. They may be broadcast, placed in bands or drilled into the soil near the roots of the plants. Very often they are applied in solution or as foliar sprays.

It should be remembered that fertilisers should never be applied in stronger doses than the strength recommended. If the fertiliser is too strong, the plant becomes dehydrated and soon collapses and dies.

Remember these

Available soil nutrients Nutrients present in a form that is available to plants

Broadcasting Scattering evenly on the surface of the soil.

Complete fertiliser A fertiliser consisting of a mixture of N.P.K. in different proportion or ratio.

Insoluble compounds	Compounds present in the soil which are not available to plants.
Nitrates	Soluble compounds derived from the mineralisation of nitrogenous substances.
Plasmolysed cells	Cells from which cell sap has been withdrawn.
Simple fertiliser	A fertiliser in which only one element is present.
Soil solution	Soil water containing dissolved mineral substances.
Trace elements	Elements required by plants in very minute quantities.
Vegetative growth	Leaf and stem development in plants.

Practical activities

1 Select two tomato plants in your garden plot and label them A and B. Feed plant A with plain clear water. Feed plant B with a saturated solution of sulphate of ammonia (dissolve as much sulphate of ammonia as is possible). Look at the plants after three to four days and record your observations.

Give reasons for any differences observed.

2 Collect samples of simple and complete inorganic fertilisers. Label, classify them and place them on your laboratory shelf.

3 Select a fruit tree in your school orchard e.g. citrus or mango that is about two years old. Remove the weeds around the plant and stir the soil along the leaf drip area. Apply 250 g of sulphate of ammonia in a band evenly on the surface of the soil along the leaf drip and soak in with a can of water.

Observe the plant 6–8 weeks later and record your observations.

4 Now read over again the chapters 'Manures and Fertilisers'. Complete the following table and the one over the page, and use them to help you grow better crops in your home and school gardens.

Fertiliser	Examples	Sources of origin	How applied	Effect on soil or on plant growth
1. Organic	a. pen manure	plant and animal	Ploughed into the soil just before planting	Improves soil physically, rich in plant nutrients, increases leaf and shoot growth
	b.			
	c.			
	d.			
	e.			
	f.			

Fertiliser	Examples	Sources of origin	How applied	Effect on soil or on plant growth
2. Inorganic	a. sulphate ammonia	Manufactured	a. Broadcast b. In solution	a. Improves vegetative growth b. Tends to make soil acid
	b.			
	c.			
	d.			
	e.			
	f.			

5 Visit the nearest garden shop and prepare a list of what commercial fertilisers are available and their prices.

Do these test exercises

1 Select the best answer from the choices given.

a A nitrogenous compound used in the preparation of animal feed is
  A sulphate of ammonia
  B urea
  C muriate of potash
  D calcium nitrate

b Which fertiliser would you recommend for use on a slightly acid soil?
  A Urea
  B Sulphate of Ammonia
  C Ammonium nitrate
  D Calcium nitrate

c The fertiliser best suited for tomato in its flowering and bearing stage is:
  A 22.11.11
  B 13.13.21
  C 5.10.5
  D 10.10.10

d A farmer fertilised his melongene plot with urea. His objective was to
  A promote vegetative growth.
  B encourage flowering and fruiting.
  C assist root development.
  D prevent deficiency diseases.

e The most suitable method of applying fertiliser to a pasture is by:
  A using fertiliser in solution.
  B band application.
  C broadcasting.
  D foliar sprays.

2 Complete the passage below by filling the blank spaces with suitable words from this list: leafy, synthesis, cell wall, green, vegetative early, needed, protoplasm, best

Nitrogen is .... in the .... of protein, the formation of .... and in the .... growth of plants. It is .... suited for .... crops, and plants in their .... stages of growth. Nitrogen helps to maintain the .... colour of the leaves of plants.

3 Explain why mixed fertilisers are in popular use.

4 Sweet peppers grown on a fertilised, well drained garden plot showed yellowing. What action should be taken to rectify this?

5 Give three examples of
  a nitrogenous fertilisers,
  b phosphatic fertilisers,
  c potash fertilisers,
  d mixed fertilisers,

6 Give two examples of fertilisers that are suited for
  a patchoi or lettuce
  b sweet potatoes
  c melongene in the flowering stage
  d pasture grasses.

7 Say how you would:
  a apply trace elements to a citrus orchard.
  b fertilise corn in a row plantation.
  c try to save a plot of lettuce that recently had a very heavy application of sulphate of ammonia.

8 Soil properties

Lesson objectives

Crops grow and thrive well on fertile soils, that is, soils that have a proper balance of air and moisture and an adequate supply of plant nutrients. The soil must not be too acid or too alkaline. The fertility of the soil depends largely upon its physical and chemical properties. On completing this lesson you should be able to:

1 identify soil properties.

2 give a simple classification of soil properties.

3 relate soil texture to soil type.

4 explain the effect of a soil 'pan' on aeration, water movement and root development in the soil.

5 explain the influence of soil properties on soil fertility.

6 explain how soil acidity and alkalinity is measured.

7 identify the causes of soil acidity.

8 describe how soil acidity is corrected.

9 perform specified experiments to demonstrate certain soil properties.

In Book One we learned about sand, clay and loam, which are our three major soil types. Soils vary in colour. Some of them are readily drained and well aerated, while others tend to be waterlogged; some are rich in plant nutrients, while others are poor. We also know that soils may be acid or alkaline.

Farmer Edward grows cabbage in his garden plot. He maintains the fertility of the soil so as to get a good cabbage crop with high yields. Let us try to find out more about soils and soil fertility.

Physical properties

A soil is considered fertile or infertile according to the **physical** and **chemical properties** which predominate. Let us consider some of these soil properties:

Colour

There are considerable variations in the colour of the soil. Surface soils of cocoa plantations or forested lands are rich in organic matter and are usually dark in colour. The sub-soil is lighter in colour. The soil on the edges of a newly dug piece of land may show red mottling. This is due to the presence of iron compounds. Limestone soils may range from light bluish to palish red in colour; swampy soils may appear grey to bluish in colour.

Texture and structure

You will remember that soil texture relates to the inorganic particles that go to make up a soil; for example, a field of sand consists of sand particles. The proportions in which the various particles exist in the soil make up the soil type. Here are the compositions of some of our commonest soil types.

Sandy soil

Soil Type	Sand	Silt	Clay
Sandy	90–95 per cent	0–5 per cent	0–5 per cent
Sandy loam	50–70 per cent	20–25 per cent	5–10 per cent
Loam	45–55 per cent	15–30 per cent	10–20 per cent
Clayey loam	25–30 per cent	35–40 per cent	20–30 per cent
Clay	20–25 per cent	25–30 per cent	30–40 per cent

A ploughed field

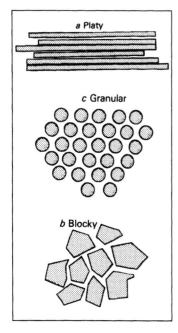

a Platy

c Granular

b Blocky

Soil structure refers to the way in which soil particles are put together to form aggregates. Look at a recently ploughed field and you will see aggregates or clumps of soil of varying sizes.

Several factors assist in aggregate formation. Moisture, organic matter and clay help to bind and cement the soil particles, whilst the activities of soil animals and micro-organisms increase soil granulation. On heavy clays the addition of lime helps to break up the soil and give it a good crumbly structure.

Soil structures vary considerably. The figures on the left show you three natural types of soil structure common under humid tropical conditions.

Farmer Edward is interested in the texture and structure of his garden soil. This helps him to practise good cultivation measures, such as tillage, drainage, irrigation, and the application of manures.

Cohesion

Cohesion relates to the ability of soil particles to cohere, that is, to stick together to form an aggregate. Sandy or gravelly soils lack cohesion, whereas moist soils containing clay and organic matter tend to cohere readily. Cohesion is important in soil structure as it assists in the formation of stable soil aggregates. You will remember that aggregation improves soil aeration and helps to control the movement of water in the soil.

Porosity

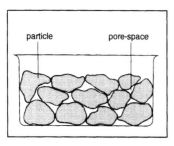

particle   pore-space

Observe the **pore spaces** between the particles in the jars.

You will notice that the sizes of the pore spaces vary according to the soil particle size; large particle size means large pore spaces and small particle size means small pore spaces. In the soil the pore spaces are filled with air and water. This is the source of the air and water taken up by the roots of plants.

You need to know that particle size influences pore size and pore size determines the air and water content of the soil as well as the rate of water movement in the soil.

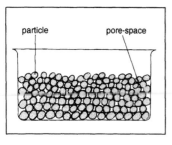

particle   pore-space

Permeability

Permeability is defined as the ability of the soil to allow water to pass through it. In the experiment below equal quantities of water were poured into equal volumes of sand, loam and clay and allowed to drain over a period of twenty-four hours.

You will observe that permeability is highest in sand and lowest in clay. The experiment also indicates that clay retains more water than sand.

Permeability and water retention in soils are related to the sizes of the soil particles and the pore spaces. A sandy soil is composed of large particles and large pore spaces. As a result it is very permeable, but retains very little water. Now make appropriate observations about loams and clays.

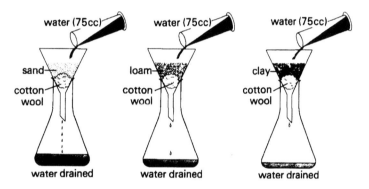

Capillarity

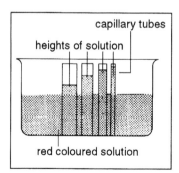

The diagram demonstrates the force of capillary attraction. The beaker is half full with a coloured solution. In this are placed vertically four pieces of narrow glass tubing of the same height but with bores of varying diameters.

Observe the natural force (or the capillary attraction) by which the water is drawn up the tube. The capillarity with which the water moves varies with the diameter of the tubes. As the tubes become narrower the capillary attraction becomes greater.

Now take a potted plant that lacks water (the soil in the pot should be practically dry) and place it in a basin of water for a period of four to five hours. Examine the soil at the top of the pot. Is it dry or moist? Say why the soil remains dry or becomes moist.

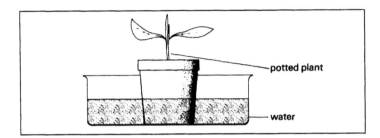

You will remember that clayey soils have very small pore spaces, known as capillary pore spaces. Water is held and moved in these spaces by means of capillary attraction. **Capillary water** is important in the soil, as this is the main source of available water for crops.

Swelling and shrinkage

The picture on this page shows you cracks (or fissures) on the soil's surface. These cracks are evident in clayey soils, especially in the dry season. During the wet season they soon disappear. Why does this happen? It is because the clay particles are very small and have the property of swelling or expanding by absorbing moisture.

In the dry season, evaporation takes place and moisture is lost from the surfaces of the clay particles. As a result they shrink and pull apart, causing large cracks in the earth.

Now think of three ways in which cracks and fissures in the soil are (a) helpful, and (b) harmful.

Other physical conditions of the soil

Surface crusting

Soil with organic manures applied

Surface crusting

Look at your garden plot after a heavy shower of rain. You will notice that the soil aggregates are broken down to form a surface crust.

A crusted soil is compact and does not readily allow water to enter. The exchange of gases in the soil is also hindered. Such conditions are unfavourable for the growth and development of roots. Say how root development is affected by surface crusting.

Farmer Edward reduces surface crusting by incorporating organic manures into the soil. He applies a mulch and keeps his plots covered with crops. After heavy showers of rain, he breaks the surface by stirring the soil.

Puddles

Farmer Edward does not plough or rotavate his field when it is damp or wet. Under these conditions ploughing or rotavating would break down the soil structure and disperse the soil particles in the soil water to form 'puddles'.

Puddled soil

The majority of garden crops cannot grow or thrive in puddled soils. However, this condition suits lagoon rice (or paddy). This crop obtains its water supply through its roots, and its air supply through its stems and leaves.

Soil compaction (pan formation)

Soil compaction takes place when soil particles are pressed together to form a hard impenetrable layer (or 'pan'). This condition occurs when the soil is cultivated, to a constant depth over a number of years. The weight of the cultivating machine and the deposits of mineral salts tend to press and bind the soil that underlies the cultivated layer.

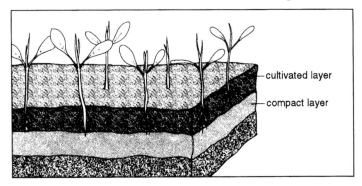

The illustration on the next page shows you how pan formation affects soil condition and plant growth.
You will notice that pan formation restricts the downward movement of water during the wet season and the upward movement in the dry season. Gas exchange in the soil and the development of the roots of plants are also affected.

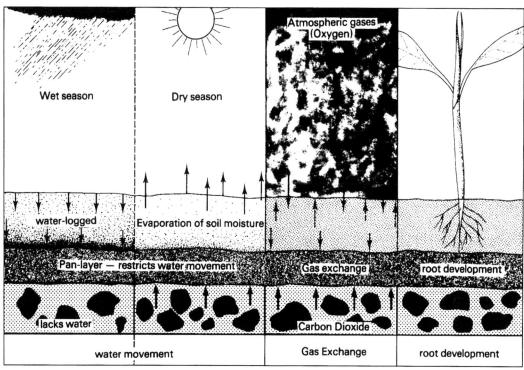

Effects of pan formation

The chemical properties of soils

You will remember that the soil is derived from organic and inorganic substances. These substances contain several chemical elements which give the soil its chemical properties. Let us look at three chemical properties of the soil.

1 Soil minerals

The soil is composed of various kinds of mineral particle. These particles vary in size. The table below shows you the chief mineral particles that make up our soil.

Mineral particle	Size
Stone or gravel	Very coarse
Sand	Coarse
Silt	Fine
Clay	Very fine

These inorganic mineral particles are derived from the parent rock, and the elements present in them depend upon the parent rock's chemical composition. These mineral are the sources from which the plants obtain most of their micro-nutrient and macro-nutrient supplies.

2 Organic matter

Organic matter is the major source of nitrogen, phosphorus, and sulphur in the soil. The organic content of soil varies with locality and climatic conditions. Minerals or clay soils may contain as much as 20 per cent organic matter, whereas the percentage in peaty or swampy soils is higher than this.

High temperature and rainfall favour the rapid decomposition of organic matter. As a result, tropic soils are quickly depleted of their organic content. This is why Farmer Edward adds organic matter regularly to his soil.

3 Soil pH – Acidity and alkalinity

Soils may be **acid**, **alkaline** or **neutral**. Acidity and alkalinity are measured by means of a special scale known as the **pH scale**. On this scale, water has a pH of 7.0 which is called neutral. Substances with pH above neutral are alkaline, while those below neutral are acid.

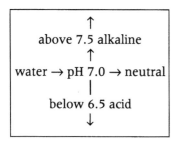

What makes the soil sour or acid?

Soil acidity results from the presence of acids in the soil, the loss of calcium by leaching, and the accumulation of hydrogen ions in the soil solution. These conditions occur when ammonium fertilisers and compost manures are applied to the soil.

How to correct soil acidity

Soil acidity is removed or corrected by the addition of the lime to the soil. Lime removes the hydrogen ions and replaces them with calcium. Farmer Edward ensures that lime is added to his soil once every two or three years.

The importance of soil pH in agriculture

Micro-organisms and higher plants respond to their chemical environment. The majority of these organisms live and thrive best at a pH of 6.5 to 7.2 – that is, from slightly acid to slightly alkaline conditions. Very few organisms can tolerate higher or lower pH conditions.

At low pH or at high pH phosphates tend to combine with iron and calcium to form insoluble phosphate compounds. As a result, phosphate deficiency may occur.

The fertile soil

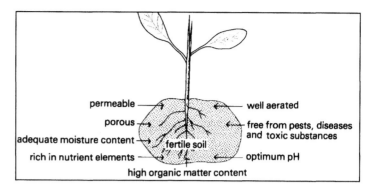

Crops grow and thrive well on fertile soil, soil that has a proper balance of air and moisture, and an adequate supply of plant nutrients. Fertile soil is neither too acid nor too alkaline, as such conditions are not favourable to most plants or to useful soil micro-organisms. It is also free from pests, diseases, and harmful substances.

Several factors operate to make a soil fertile. Look at the diagram on this page and say how these factors are related to the physical and chemical properties of the soil.

Summary

Soil fertility is largely dependent upon the physical and chemical properties of the soil.

The physical properties of the soil relate to soil colour, texture and structure, cohesion, porosity, permeability, capillarity, swelling and shrinkage and other soil conditions like surface crusting, puddling and soil compaction.

Variations in soil colour are due mainly to the presence of organic matter and to the presence of iron and limestone compounds. Soil colour also varies with locality.

Texture and structure are associated factors. Texture relates to soil particles and structure, the way in which the particles are put together to form soil aggregates.

Texture determines soil type, size of pore space, soil water content and the movement of water in the soil. Soils with large pore spaces are well aerated, well drained but retain little water, whereas soils with small capillary pore spaces hold less air but contain available soil water for plant use. There must be a good balance of soil air and soil water for good plant growth. Surface crusting, puddling and soil compaction generally have detrimental effects on plant growth and these conditions should be avoided.

The chemical properties of the soil take into account the inorganic substances present in the soil, the organic content of the soil and the soil pH. The inorganic mineral particles are the sources from which plants obtain their micro- and macro-elements. The organic matter present is also a source of nutrients but plays a greater role in soil aggregation, water retention and the development of soil micro-organisms.

Soil pH relates to soil acidity and alkalinity. Soils may be acid, neutral or alkaline. A soil with a pH of 7.0 is neutral; below this the soil is acid, and above, it is alkaline. Most plants thrive best in soils with a pH range of 6.5 to 7.2.

Soil acidity is corrected by the use of lime.

It is important that the fertility of the soil is maintained in order to promote healthy plant growth and to obtain good yields and good quality crops.

Remember these

Acid soils	Soils with pH below 7.0.
Alkaline soils	Soils with pH above 7.0.
Capillary soil water	Water present in the capillary pore spaces.
Chemical properties	Properties associated with the organic and inorganic particles of the soil.
Neutral soils	Soils with a pH of 7.0.
Permeability	The ability of the soil to allow water to pass through it.
pH scale	The scale on which soil acidity and alkalinity is measured.
Physical properties	Properties related to the physical characteristics of the soil.
Pore spaces	The spaces between the soil particles.
Retentivity	The capacity of the soil to hold water.

Practical activities

1 Cohesion

Get four containers and label them A, B, C and D. Place the following materials in the containers:

A Dry river-sand   B Damp river-sand   C Damp mixture of river-sand and pen-manure   D Damp mixture of river-sand and clay

Take a handful of material from each container and squeeze it in the palm of your hand. Did it 'cohere' or stick together to form a ball? Complete this table.

Soil material	Cohesion	No cohesion	Did cohesion continue for the next hour (Yes or No)

Which soil showed no cohesion? Why?
Which soil showed continued cohesion? Why?
How does the addition of organic matter help aggregate formation in sandy soils?

2 Permeability

Get three large funnels and plug them with cotton wool.

Fill the funnels with equal quantities of sand, loam, and clay. The soil must be air dried and finely powdered. Pour 75 cc of water into each soil type and allow to drain.

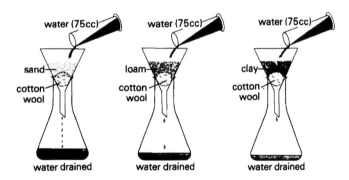

Record the following observations:

Observation	Sand	Loam	Clay
a. The time taken for the first drop of water to drip from the funnel	min.	min.	min.
b. The quantity of water drained out of the soil after 24 hours.	cc	cc	cc

From the experiment, complete this chart.

Soil	Particle size	Size of pore space	Permeability	Water retention
Loam				

Which soil is most permeable?

Which soil retains most water?

Why does a loam retain more water than sand?

Why is a loam more readily drained than clay?

3 Soil pH – acidity and alkalinity

Here is an experiment for you to do. Get six test-tubes and label them A, B, C, D, E and F. Pour equal quantities of the following substances into the labelled test-tubes.

A 20 ml of distilled water.

B 20 ml dilute hydrochloric acid } acid

C 20 ml dilute acetic acid

D 20 ml calcium hydroxide } alkaline or basic

E 20 ml sodium hydroxide

F 20 ml water

Test the rection of the substances to red litmus paper and blue litmus paper. Record your observations in the table:

Test-tubes	Substance in test-tubes	Reaction to	
		red litmus	blue litmus
A	Distilled water		
B	Dilute H Cl Acid		
C	Dilute Acetic Acid		
D	Calcium Hydroxide		
E	Sodium Hydroxide		
F	Water		

From your observations tell what reaction (a) acids have on blue litmus, (b) alkaline substances have on red litmus, and (c) water has on red and blue litmus.

4 Acid soils and alkaline soils

Soils may be acid, alkaline, or neutral. Take a 5g sample of each of the following air-dried powdered soils. Use a dropper and pour some dilute hydrochloric acid on each sample. Did you see an effervescence (release of gases)? The greater the effervescence, the more alkaline the substance. Record your observations.

Soil samples	Treatment	Observation a.Heavy effervescence b.Slight c.No
a. Sand	Test each	
b. Loam	sample with	
c. Clay	4–5 drops of	
d. Limestone	dil. HCl acid	

Which soil showed the greatest reaction to dilute hydrochloric acid? Is this soil acid or alkaline?

How can a farmer use this test to help him with his soil management?

Do these test exercises

1 Consider these statements carefully. State whether they are *true* or *false*.

a Sandy soils retain less water than clayey soils.

b Capillary soil water is not available to plants.

c Mulching increases surface crusting.

d The chemical composition of soils may vary from place to place.

e Red mottling in clayey soils indicates the presence of iron compounds.

2 Select the best answer from the choices given.

a Which of these is not considered a physical property of the soil?

A Soil texture and structure.

B Capillary pore spaces.

C Inorganic soil substances.

D Surface crusting.

b Water logging is likely to be most prevalent in:

A sands

B clays

C loams

D sandy loams

c Organic matter is a major source of:

A nitrogen

B phosphorus

C sulphur

D all of the above

d Most plants thrive well in a pH range of:

A 4.4 to 5.4

B 5.5 to 6.4

C 6.5 to 7.2

D 7.3 to 8.2

e Surface crusting could be reduced by:

A more frequent use of sprinkler irrigation.

B adding organic manures to the soil.

C constructing proper drains.

D deep ploughing the soil.

3 Say why

a sandy soils are readily drained.

b farmers avoid ploughing their fields under wet or damp conditons.

c paddy or rice can grow in puddled soils.

d organic matter must be added regularly in tropical soils.

e cohesion is greater in clay soils than in sandy soils.

4 Say how

a soil compaction or 'pan' formation could be avoided.

b cracks in the earth's surface may be harmful to plants.

c soil acidity is corrected.

d surface crusting hinders root-development.

e pore size affect drainage in soils.

5 In your own words say what you mean by

a parent rocks.

b capillary soil water.

c a waterlogged soil.

d an alkaline soil.

e available soil water.

6 Say how the following operations improve the fertility of the soil.

a The addition of organic matter to the soil.

b Breaking the surface-crust after a shower of rain.

c The addition of lime to the soil.

9 Soil cultivation methods

Lesson objectives

Tillage and drainage are two very important soil cultivation practices. They improve the physical condition of the soil making it more fertile for crop production. On completing this lesson you should be able to:

1 explain the terms tillage and drainage.

2 identify methods of tillage and drainage.

3 explain how tillage and drainage improve soil fertility.

4 give reasons for good crop growth on well drained soils.

5 select appropriate methods of tillage and drainage to suit prevailing conditions.

6 explain how deep drainage increases root room.

7 describe how underground drains are constructed.

8 prepare a model to demonstrate contour drainage.

9 perform an experiment to demonstrate the effect of waterlogging on crop growth.

Farmers increase the fertility of their soil by cultivating it. They till and drain the soil in order to improve its physical condition and to make plant nutrients more available.

Tillage

Tillage is the process of digging or turning the soil. This could be done manually by using a garden fork or by machines such as a power driven hand rotavator or by a plough pulled by a tractor.

How tillage helps to make the soil fertile

Here is a plot of land that was recently tilled and prepared for planting crops. During the process of tillage the soil is broken into clumps or aggregates. The subsoil is exposed to weathering which activates nutrient elements, making them available to plants. Soil insects and other harmful organisms are also exposed to the surface, where they are destroyed by birds, lizards and frogs.

In the process of tillage weeds and plant residues are turned into the soil. These decay to form organic matter which is a source of plant nutrients and which helps in the retention of soil water. Organic matter is also essential for the growth and development of useful soil organisms.

Tillage helps to loosen the soil, increase the infiltration of water and improve aeration. As a result the roots grow and spread deeper into the soil.

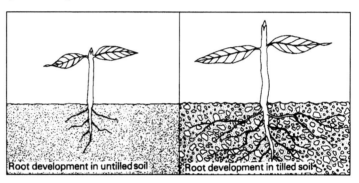

Root development in untilled soil Root development in tilled soil

Depth of tillage

Farmer Edward tills his cabbage field with a rotavator (bottom left) and his sugar-cane field with a disc plough (bottom).

The depth of tillage depends upon the nature of the soil and the type of crop that is to be grown. Heavy clays become waterlogged and compact very quickly. They need deep tillage in order to keep them loose and readily

drained. Sands and loams are porous, free-draining, and do not need deep tillage.

Some crops, like corn and sugar-cane, have deep-rooting systems. Such crops thrive better on lands that are ploughed deeply. Vegetable crops lke cabbage, lettuce, and patchoi are shallow-rooted and grow quite well on soils that are rotavated to a depth of 15 cm to 20 cm.

Tillage on hillsides

Rills, or water channels, on a hillside

Look at the movement of water after a shower of rain. You will observe that the water runs down the slopes forming rills and gullies. The surface soil is washed away, leaving the poorer soil behind. As a result crop growth is retarded and production falls.

Tillage on hillsides should be done on the contour, that is, across the slopes (as we see in the picture below). This helps to break the downhill flow and reduce the speed of the slope water, thereby reducing soil erosion.

Say why you think the practice of contour tillage is important in many Caribbean islands.

Do you know what is meant by the soil's tilth? Can tillage affect the soil's **tilth**? It is the coarseness or fineness of the soil aggregates. A good tilth is one that is not too fine or too coarse. It must be crumbly in nature, with a continuous system of pores leading from the surface to the **water table**, that is, the depth at which you get water when you dig the soil.

Tillage should not be done when the weather conditions are too dry or too wet. When the soil is rotavated under very dry conditions, the soil aggregates break down to form a dust mulch. Soil particles are easily blown away by the wind, and with the first rain the dust mulch cakes up to form a compact surface crust. When the soil is very wet soil aggregates disintegrate to form puddles.

What effect does surface crusting have on soil air and soil water?

Drainage

The farmer in the picture on the left is draining his garden. Why is **drainage** necessary in a garden?

You will remember that plants need an optimum supply of soil water. When soil water is short, plants wilt and die, whereas a badly drained or **waterlogged soil** lacks aeration. In poorly drained soils the roots of plants are not able to grow and absorb their nutrient supplies properly.

Why plants grow better on well drained soils

Plants grow and thrive best in soils that are deep, free draining and well aerated. Drainage removes excess surface water as well as water occupying the air spaces in the soil, that is, the large pore-spaces along the soil profile. As a result, soil aeration is increased and more oxygen is provided for the development of root hairs, the absorption of mineral salts, and the activities of useful soil micro-organisms.

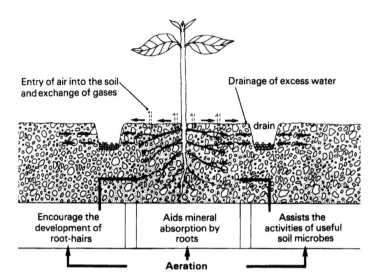

How good drainage helps plant growth

Drainage increases root-room

All plants need adequate **root-room**, that is, a well-drained permeable soil to root depth, for good root development. Some crops, like coffee, cocoa, and citrus, have deep roots and can only grow on low-lying areas if the lands are well drained. Deep drains provide greater depth of soil for root development. (See diagram below).

Deep drainage lowers the water table by removing excess water at a lower depth in the soil, increasing the depth at which root growth and development can take place.

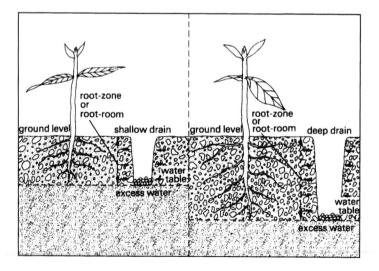

How the soil is drained

Natural drainage
Sandy or limestone soils are very porous. They have natural drainage. Water permeates the soil to enter underground water channels. Such soils are well aerated but they suffer water shortages during dry spells.

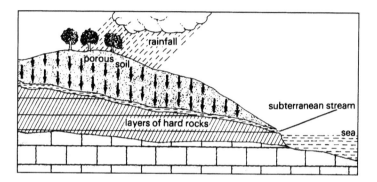

Hillsides or slopes that are impermeable to water are drained by means of **surface run-off**. When it is very wet the removal of surface soil, or erosion, may occur.

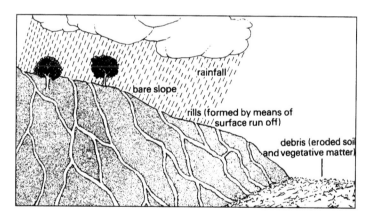

Artificial drainage
Artificial drainage by means of open ditches or underground drains, is necessary on heavy clays and loams.

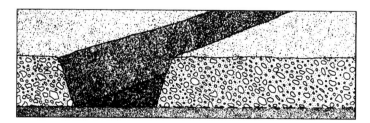

An open ditch

Open ditches are used in plantations, pastures, and vegetable fields. The depth and width of these drains depend upon the soil type and the crop. Heavy soil with deep-rooted crops must be deeply drained, whereas shallow drains suit lighter soil types or shallow-rooted crops.

Open drains should have a good **gradient**, that is, a drop along the length of the drain and must be sufficiently large to allow the flow of water. They should be kept free from weeds and clumps of soil, as these may block the flow.

Closed or underground drains are deep ditches filled with porous materials such as stones or perforated hollow tiles, which allow the movement of excess water in water-logged soils. These drains are very efficient, but they are easily blocked by soil if they are not properly constructed.

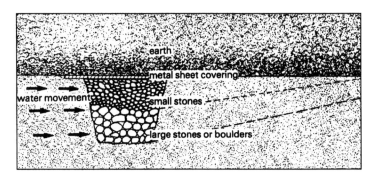

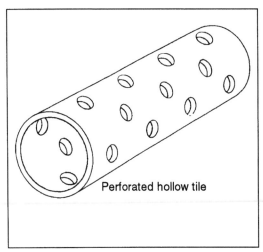

Perforated hollow tile

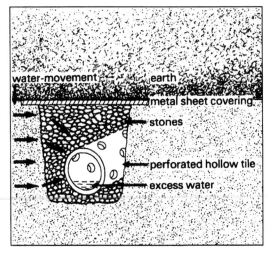

Carefully observe the construction of open drains and underground drains.

Which type of drain is cheaper to construct?

Which type of drain is in greater use?

Why do farmers prefer to use open drains in their gardens?

Drainage on hillsides

You will remember that on hillsides erosion is rapid. **Contour drains**, that is, drains across the slopes, help to break the flow and decrease the speed of water. As a result, more water soaks into the soil and erosion is reduced.

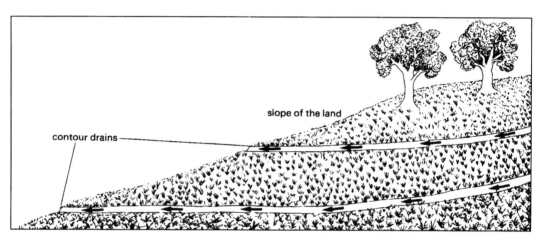

slope of the land

contour drains

Summary

Tillage and drainage are two major soil cultivation practices. These operations improve the physical condition of the soil and maintain its fertility.

Tillage is described as the process of digging and turning the soil. It can be done manually by use of a garden fork or mechanically by a machine such as a tractor. Tillage helps to improve soil fertility in the following ways.

1 The subsoil is exposed to weathering which activates nutrient elements, making them available to plants.

2 Soil insects and other harmful organisms are exposed to the surface where they are destroyed by predators.

3 Weed and plant residues are turned into the soil. These decompose to form organic matter which enriches the soil, improves the retention of water in the soil and facilitates the development of useful soil micro-organisms.

4 Tillage loosens the soil, increases the infiltration of water and improves aeration. As a result, roots grow and spread deeper into the soil.

Tillage is best done when it is not too wet or too dry. The depth of tillage depends upon the soil type and the crop to be grown. It must be remembered, too, that on hillsides tillage must be done on the contours so as to reduce erosion and to allow more water to enter the soil.

Drainage is the removal of excess water from the soil. Aeration is improved and more oxygen is made available for the development of root hairs, the absorption of mineral salts and the activities of useful soil micro-organisms. By increasing the depth of drains, the water table is lowered and more root room is provided for plants.

Drainage takes place naturally, especially in porous soils where water permeates and moves freely down through the soil. On hillsides, water runs along the slopes forming gullies.

On heavy soil types such as clays artificial drains are constructed. These may be of the open ditch type or closed underground drains, which are deep ditches filled with porous materials such as stones or perforated hollow tiles.

On hillsides, contour drains should be constructed. These help to reduce erosion and increase the infiltration of water into the soil.

Remember these

Contour drains	Drains constructed on the contours, that is, across the slopes on hillsides.
Drainage	The removal of excess water from the soil.
Gradient	A drop along the length of a drain, allowing water to flow.
Root room	A well drained permeable soil to root depth.
Subsoil	Soil that is 15–20 cm below the surface.
Surface run off	Water which runs off along the surface of the ground.
Tillage	The process of digging and turning the soil.
Tilth	The state of coarseness or fineness of the soil aggregates.
Waterlogged soil	Soil in which the pore spaces are filled with water.
Water table	The depth at which you get water when you dig the soil.

Practical activities

1 Construct an open drain 5 m long, 30 cm wide and 15 cm deep. Give a gentle gradient along the length of the drain. Comment on the movement of water after rain.

2 Get two pots for potting plants and label them A and B. Fill pot A with potting soil, ensuring proper drainage in the pot. Fill pot B with similar potting soil, but ensure

there is no drainage in the pot. Sow corn seeds in both pots A and B and allow to grow.

Apply 500 cc of plain water to each pot once per day. Make observations on the plant growth at the end of three weeks. State reasons for the differences observed.

3 While ploughing your school garden plot collect as many soil organisms as you can find. Identify them and state how they are useful or harmful in agriculture.

4 Use a quantity of moist clay and construct a model of a hillside showing contour drainage. Explain why contour drains are recommended on hillsides.

Do these test exercises

1 **Consider these statements carefully. State whether they are *true* or *false*.**

a Weathering activates nutrient elements in the soil.

b Waterlogging does not affect soil aeration.

c It is less costly to construct underground drains than open drains.

d Deep drainage increases root room.

e Ploughing is best done after heavy showers of rain.

2 **Select the best answer from the choices given.**

a Deep tillage is necessary in the cultivation of

A lettuce

B cucumber

C corn

D cauliflower

b To increase root room a farmer should construct

A deep drains

B shallow drains

C open drains

D contour drains

c Subterranean streams are generally associated with

A clayey soils

B sandy or limestone soils

C loamy soils

D any soil type

d On low lying lands crop growth is best improved by

A regular application of fertilisers.

B applying a surface mulch.

C incorporating organic manures in the soil.

D deep ploughing and deep drainage.

e Soil aeration provides oxygen for

(i) root hair development

(ii) the absorption of mineral salts

(iii) the activities of useful soil organisms

In the statements above

A (i) alone is correct

B (ii) alone is correct.

C (iii) alone is correct.

D (i), (ii) and (iii) are all correct.

3 **Explain in your own words**

a Gradient of a drain

b Rills and gullies on hillsides

c Water-table

d Root zone or root-room

4 **Say why**

a sandy soils have natural drainage

b sugar-cane lands must be ploughed deeply

c too fine a soil tilth is not desirable

d a drain should have a gradient

e farmers prefer to construct open drains in their garden plots

5 **Say how**

a deep drains increase root-room.

b tillage controls weeds.

c contour drains prevent erosion.

d drainage improves aeration.

e an underground drain is constructed.

6 **Look at the soil in your school garden. Does it need shallow drains or deep drains? Give reasons for your answer.**

7 **Write a short paragraph saying how drainage enables plants to make better use of nutrients in the soil.**

8 **Some corn planted on low-lying lands showed yellowing. What do you think was responsible for this? What should a farmer do to prevent such yellowing of corn?**

10 The conservation and maintenance of soil and soil water

Lesson objectives

Soil and soil water are two major agricultural resources which must be conserved and maintained. There are several soil cultivation and irrigation practices used by farmers to ensure the conservation of soil and soil water.

On completing this lesson you should be able to:

1 explain why erosion takes place more rapidly on hill-sides than on low lands.

2 identify techniques of conserving soil and water on sloping lands.

3 list the advantages of soil and water conservation in crop production.

4 describe two soil conservation practices used on hill-sides.

5 list five methods of irrigation.

6 describe two types of irrigation practice.

7 select irrigation methods appropriate to (a) crop type and (b) soil type.

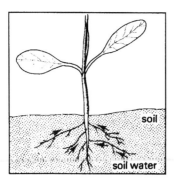

The soil is the chief medium on which farmers grow their crops. Soil water is needed in the formation of soil solution from which plants obtain their water and mineral supplies. Soil and soil water are two important agricultural resources which must be conserved and maintained.

The picture on page 111 shows soil **erosion**. You will remember that erosion is the removal of surface soil by wind or by water. This surface or top-soil is rich in organic matter and plant nutrients. Crops grown on eroded land show poor growth with low yields and low quality produce. Give reasons for this poor crop growth.

Eroded soil

In a prolonged dry season, there is often a shortage of soil water and crops tend to wilt and die. Under such conditions **irrigation** becomes necessary.

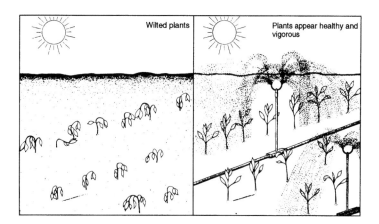

Farmer Perez is concerned about the conservation of soil and soil water. These resources are affected by the changes in seasonal weather conditions, thc kind of crops grown, and the cultivation method employed. Let us see the cultivation practices adopted by Farmer Perez.

Soil and water conservation on hillsides

We have learned that erosion and run-off take place more rapidly on bare steep hillsides during the wet season. Here are some of the control measures practised by Farmer Perez.

Contour tillage and drainage

In Chapter 9 we looked at erosion on hillsides and how this could be reduced by means of contour tillage and drainage. You will recall that these practices reduce the speed and movement of surface run-off. As a result less erosion takes place and more water infiltrates the soil.

Terracing

Terracing is another means of controlling erosion and conserving surface run-off on sloping lands. Look at the figure below and see how a bench terrace is constructed.

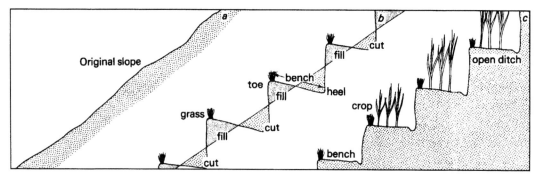

Notice how soil is cut at the heel end and thrown at the toe end to form a bench. The bench slopes towards the heel and the water runs across the bench along the heel to an open ditch. A deep-rooting grass is planted along the toe. This helps to bind the soil and prevent landslides. Crops are grown on the benches.

Terracing is a systematic means of intercepting and diverting surface run off. The construction of terraces helps to conserve soil and water, and it makes cropping operations easier. However, the operation is very costly and farmer Perez will crop on the hillside only if good flat lands are not available.

Contour strip cropping

In this system, crops are planted on strips of land which run on the contours at right-angles to the slopes. A strip of ground with crops on it is alternated with a strip on which grasses, legumes, or a mixture of both is planted.

The grass or legume strip acts as a barrier to the movement of soil and water. Strip cropping lends itself to good crop-rotation: after a period of time the grass and legume strips are planted with crops and the strips which had borne crops are planted with grasses and legumes.

Contour strip cropping

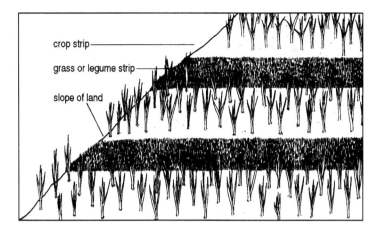

Use of bunds

Farmer Perez finds it convenient to use the trunks and branches of felled trees, or the stubble of old crops, to form bunds across the slopes. These bunds alternate with strips of ground on which crops are planted.

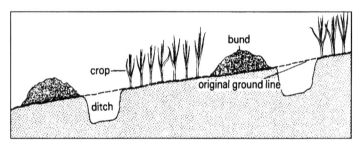

On rocky hillsides bunds are often built from loose rocks cleared from the land. Study the diagram above and find out how bunds help to conserve soil and water on hillsides.

Use of vegetative covers and tree crops

The picture below shows you a steep hillside planted with tree crops. Hillsides may also be planted with a cover-crop, which covers the ground completely, like kudzu.

Study the diagram below. It explains how trees and other cover crops help to conserve soil and water.

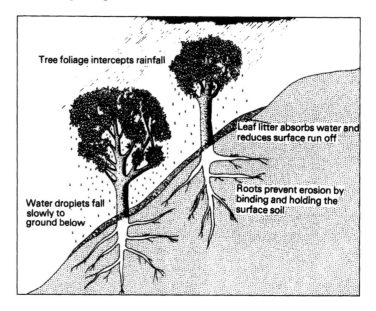

Tree foliage intercepts rainfall

Leaf litter absorbs water and reduces surface run off

Roots prevent erosion by binding and holding the surface soil

Water droplets fall slowly to ground below

Trees and vegetative cover-crops help to conserve soil and water on hillsides. The foliage of plants intercepts raindrops and prevents them from hitting and splashing the soil. The decomposition of leaf litter adds organic matter to the soil, and this absorbs and retains water. As a result surface run-off is reduced. The roots of plants hold and bind the soil and so prevent erosion.

The conservation and maintenance of soil water in the dry season

During the dry season, soil water is often in short supply. However, the trees and crops in Farmer Perez' garden never wilt. He conserves and maintains water in the soil by means of the following garden operations.

Mulching

What is mulch? When and why do we mulch?

This picture shows you a mulched citrus tree. A mulch is a surface dressing of soil, manure, straw, leaf litter, sawdust, coffee-hauls and any other available material.

Mulching is done just before the dry season begins. The mulch is about 8 cm thick and is placed around the plant at a distance of 60 cm away from the stem. Mulching is especially important for young trees and shallow-rooted plants. What reasons can you give for this?

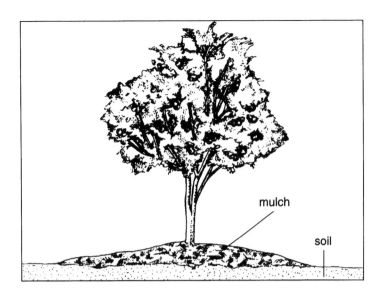

A mulch reduces evaporation caused by drying winds and controls variation in day and night temperatures. The moist conditions under a mulch favour the activities of micro-organisms and small animals. As a result, the structure and permeability of the soil is improved.

The addition of organic matter

Organic matter improves the permeability of soils and increases their ability to absorb and retain water. Farmer Perez ensures that there is sufficient organic matter in his garden soil by ploughing in pen-manure, compost, and other decaying organic substances.

Irrigation practices

Farmer Perez provides water for his crops in the drought period by means of irrigation. Water supplied by irrigation must meet the **optimum water requirement** of the crop, that is, just the amount of water that the crop needs. When inadequate amounts of soil water are available, low yields and poor quality produce result. Crops may even wilt and die. Excess irrigation is harmful, as it breaks down the soil structure and causes surface crusting. In sandy or porous soils heavy nutrient losses occur as a result of leaching.

Irrigation frequency

How often should our crops be irrigated? This will depend on the soil type, the crops grown, and their stages of growth.

Think carefully and say why more frequent irrigation is needed (a) on sandy soils than on clays and loams, (b) on soils with low organic matter content than on soils with high organic matter content, (c) for shallow-rooted crops than for deep-rooted crops and (d) in the early stages of plant growth than in their late stages of growth.

In the Caribbean, an average of 100 mm of rainfall per month, or 25 mm per week is adequate. In the dry season most farmers irrigate their crops to root depth, that is, to the depth to which the roots grow and spread in the soil, once every seven to ten days.

How crops are irrigated

Irrigation is only possible in the presence of a good water supply obtained from rivers, lakes and dams. Crops are irrigated in several ways. In this book we are going to look at five methods of irrigation in common use, (a) overhead irrigation, (b) channel irrigation, (c) furrow irrigation, (d) drip irrigation and (e) flooding.

Overhead irrigation involves the application of water by means of overhead sprinklers and jet sprays. Water is pumped through pipelines to orchards, vegetable crops, and pastures. Name the components or items needed to set up an overhead sprinkler irrigation unit.

Can this system be used both on lowlands and hillsides? In what ways is this system advantageous to a farmer?

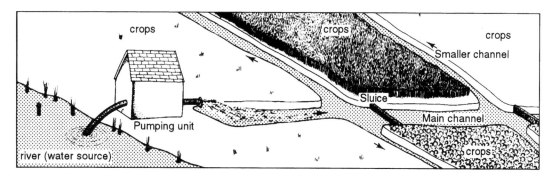

The picture above shows you the irrigation of a vegetable field by means of water channels. Water is pumped from a river or lake into a large or main channel. From the main channel smaller channels filled with water radiate into the cultivated field. Water control in the channels is maintained by **sluices** or water-gates. Why is this system of irrigation best suited for gently sloping or flat land?

Furrow irrigation works efficiently in **row crops** like corn and tomatoes, or in orchard crops like citrus. Water from a ditch is fed into furrows from one end of the field and allowed to flow to the opposite end. In the process, water diffuses laterally through the soil to the roots of the plants. In localities where water is in limited supply **drip irrigation**, also known as trickle irrigation, is practised. Water is brought in by **perforated pipe** lines and allowed to drip or trickle down to the roots of the plants where the water is needed most. The water is regulated by a control system.

Periodically fertilisers are added to the water so that the plants are fertilised during the process of irrigation.

Furrow irrigation

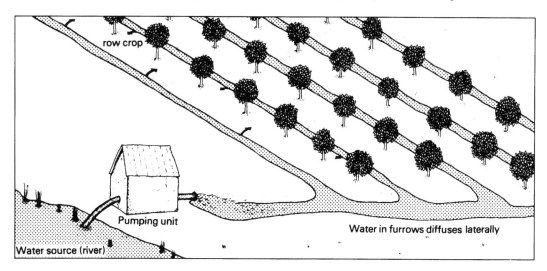

Drip irrigation

Flooding is often used on low-level land planted with crops like sugar-cane, rice, or corn. Water is lifted from a river or dam and the entire surface of the land is flooded for 12 to 24 hours. Sandy soils and loams are irrigated for shorter periods than clay loams or clays. Why?

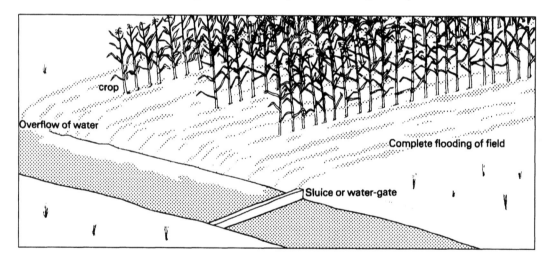

crop

Overflow of water

Complete flooding of field

Sluice or water-gate

Summary

Soil and soil water are two important agricultural resources which must be conserved and maintained. These resources are affected by the seasonal changes in weather conditions, the kind of crops grown and the cultivation methods used.

Soil conservation is especially important on hillsides. During the rainy season erosion takes place and valuable topsoil is lost as a result of surface run-off. Some of the measures adopted to reduce run-off and erosion are contour tillage and drainage, terracing, construction of bunds and the use of vegetative cover and tree crops.

The main purpose of these control measures is to break

the speed and the force of surface run-off, thereby reducing erosion and allowing more water to infiltrate the soil. In addition, the remains of tree and cover crops produce organic matter which absorbs and retains water.

Soil water is often in short supply during the dry season. The conservation of water in the soil is achieved by applying a surface mulch or by incorporating organic matter into the soil. Mulching reduces evaporation whilst the organic matter absorbs and retains water.

Under very dry conditions, irrigation becomes necessary. Crops are irrigated once every seven to ten days by use of overhead sprinklers or by other methods such as channel irrigation, furrow irrigation, drip irrigation and flooding.

It is important to remember that water supplied by irrigation must meet the optimum water requirement of crops.

Remember these

Contour strip cropping	Alternating crops with legumes or grasses on strips of land which run on the contours at right angles to the slopes.
Erosion	Removal of surface soil by wind or by water.
Irrigation	This is the process of introducing water into the land to meet the requirements of crops.
Mulching	A surface dressing of organic material designed to reduce the evaporation of soil water.
Optimum water requirement	Just the amount of water required.
Perforated pipes	Pipes with perforations to allow water to pass through.
Row crops	Crops best suited for cultivation in rows, for example corn.
Sluice	Water gates used in furrow irrigation to regulate the flow.
Terracing	Construction of terraces or benches on hillsides for the purpose of growing crops.
Vegetative cover	A crop, mainly legume, planted to cover or protect the soil.

Practical activities

1 Select a two year old citrus or mango plant in your school orchard. Clean around the plant to a distance of 60 cm away from the stem and then apply a surface mulch of organic material 8 cm thick.

  Explain how this mulch conserves water in the soil.

2 Draw a diagram to illustrate strip cropping. Say how strip cropping helps to conserve soil and water on hillsides.

3 Carefully study the diagram in this lesson on 'drip irrigation'. Collect the materials and equipment needed and set up a model to demonstrate the process of irrigation by

the drip method. State two benefits in favour of the farmer if he chooses to use this system of irrigation.

4 Grow three rows of corn on a garden plot and irrigate by furrow irrigation. Say how the water reaches the roots.

5 Establish a cover crop like bodi beans on one of your school garden plots using a planting distance of 30 cm in and between rows. Observe rainfall on the foliage. Explain how crop cover helps to conserve soil and soil water.

Do these test exercises

1 **Select the best answer from the choices given.**

a Crops should be irrigated to meet their 'optimum water requirements'. This means that the crops should be given

  A a regular supply of water

  B water at periodic intervals

  C just the right amount of water

  D water only when it is necessary

b Which group of crops is best suited for cultivation on hillsides?

  A Cassava, yam, sweet potato

  B Citrus, mango, sapodilla

  C tomato, melongene, sweet pepper

  D Cabbage, patchoi, celery

c Surface crusting takes place as a result of

  A poor soil aeration

  B rapid infiltration of soil water

  C limited amounts of soil organic matter

  D a breakdown in soil structure

d Mulching of orchard crops should be done

  A just before the dry season begins

  B at the end of the dry season

  C during the wet season

  D all through the year

e The method of irrigation most suitable for low lying level lands is

  A the use of overhead sprinklers.

  B flooding of the land.

  C channel irrigation.

  D furrow irrigation.

2 **Complete the passage below by filling the blank spaces with words from this list:**

irrigation, temperatures, soil, evaporation, structure, favours, erosion, variation, animals, micro-organisms.

A mulch reduces .... caused by drying winds and controls .... in day and night .... The moistened condition under a mulch .... the activities of .... and small .... As a result, the .... and permeability of the .... is improved.

3 **Say how erosion is controlled on hillsides by:**

a The foliage of trees.

b The roots of plants.

c Leaf-litter on the surface of the ground.

d Tillage and drainage on the contour.

e Contour strip cropping.

4 **Tell what type of irrigation is best suited for the following crops and explain why:**

a Rice or paddy.

b Vegetable leaf crops.

c Corn.

d Tomatoes.

e Sugar-cane.

f Pastures on level lands.

5 **Tell why:**

a Shallow-rooted crops need more regular irrigation than deep rooted crops.

b Erosion is greater on hillsides than on lowlands.

c Cultivated field-plots should not be flooded for very long periods.

d Crops should be irrigated to root depth.

e Crop growth is slow during the dry season.

6 **Name two cover crops that are grown on hillsides. How do these crops help to conserve soil and moisture on the hillside?**

7 **In your own words say how you would mulch a citrus tree. How does mulching benefit a citrus plant?**

8 **Look at your school garden plots. Say whether they are properly constructed or not. Give reasons for your answer.**

11

Livestock management–general principles

Lesson objectives

The main types of livestock reared by farmers in the Caribbean are cattle, pigs, goats, sheep, poultry birds and rabbits. Livestock farmers obtain their incomes from the sales of livestock and livestock products. On completing this lesson you should be able to:

1 Identify some breeds of livestock and understand the purposes for which livestock are reared.

2 List the factors that should be considered when constructing an animal house.

3 List the points that should be borne in mind when selecting animals for breeding.

4 Describe the management practices for livestock.

5 Describe how to attend to a young animal at birth.

6 State the economic importance of livestock production in agriculture.

In Book One you were introduced to farm animals. Animals domesticated and reared by farmers for their use are called **livestock**. The main types of livestock reared on farms are cattle, pigs, goats, sheep, poultry, and rabbits.

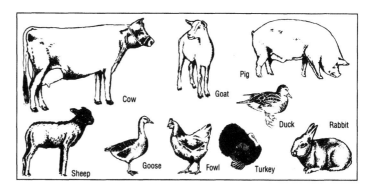

Horses, mules and donkeys are also found on some farms but these are not reared on a **commercial** scale.

Beekeeping and the rearing of fresh water fish and prawns are also a part of our livestock industry.

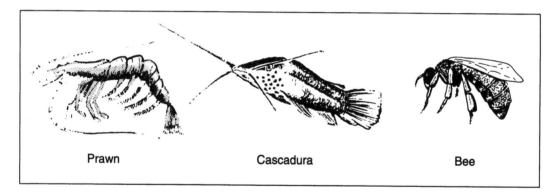

A livestock farmer depends upon the sales of his livestock and products for his **income**. The extent of his income is generally determined by the yield and the quality of the products coming from the farm. These two factors are influenced mainly by the selection of suitable animals and the level of care and management given to the animals by the farmer.

Selection of suitable animals

In selecting livestock these factors should be considered.

1 The purpose for which the animal is reared.

The table on the next page gives you a list of animals and the purposes for which they are reared. Study it carefully. It will help you to understand more about the selection of animals to suit your purposes.

Animals	Purposes
Cattle	meat, milk, processed dairy products hides and work (oxen and buffalo)
Goats and sheep	Meat, milk, wool, hair, hides
Pigs	Meat and meat products
Poultry birds	Meat, eggs, sports (game bird)
Rabbits	Meat, pelt, shows and exhibitions
Horses	Work, sport (Horse racing)
Mules and donkeys	Work
Fresh water fishes	Meat, manufactured fish products, live fish for aquarium
Prawns	Meat
Bees	Honey, wax, honey and wax products

On some farms animals are reared only for **breeding** purposes. On these farms specially selected male and female animals are bred, that is, mated to produce young animals in the case of cows and pigs or hatching eggs in poultry birds. These young animals or hatching eggs are sold to other farmers to improve their livestock or to assist in their production programmes.

2 Selection of suitable breeds

A farmer should select the breed of animal that is best suited for his production purposes. When we speak of a breed, we refer to a group of animals that possess features or characteristics that are common to that particular group, for example, Holstein cattle are generally black and white in colour, triangular in shape (that is, broad at the hind parts and narrow to the front), give high milk yield and are usually quiet and docile.

The pictures on the next page show some breeds of cattle, pig and goat. You can only observe the external body features of these animals.

Large white

Holstein

Anglo–Nubian

Berkshire

Zebu

Saanen

There are several breeds of animals reared by livestock farmers. The table below shows you some of the major breeds of animals commonly found in the Caribbean.

Animals	Breeds
Cattle	Holstein, Zebu, Jamaica Hope, Jamaica Red
Goat	Saanen, British Alpine, Anglo-Nubian, Toggenberg
Sheep	Barbados Black belly, Blackhead Persian
Pig	Large white, Landrace, Hampshire, Berkshire
Poultry (layers)	Leghorn, Golden Comet, Rhode Island Red
Rabbit	Flemish Giant, Belgian Hares, New Zealand White

Cross breeds

Some farmers practise **cross-breeding**, that is, the mating of animals belonging to two different breeds. For example, a Holstein bull is mated with a Zebu cow to produce offspring that will possess certain desirable characteristics of both breeds. The Holstein breed is noted for its high milk yield whilst the Zebu is well known for its adaptability to hot conditions and its resistance to tropical diseases. The offspring of the Holstein-Zebu cross is likely to give higher milk yields than the Zebu and to be better adapted to tropical conditions than the Holstein, which thrives and performs best under temperate conditions.

Animal functions

An animal is often described according to the function it serves. For example, the Holstein breed is described as a dairy animal because it is reared mainly for milk.

The Jamaica Red is a meat or beef animal because it is reared for meat.

The Leghorn is a **layer** because its main purpose is to lay eggs and the Vantress Cross is a **broiler** bird kept for meat. Now find out what the following mean: (a) wool type sheep; (b) dual–purpose goat; (c) working animal.

Leghorn

Selection of animals for breeding

Many farmers breed animals on their farms in order to maintain their livestock programmes. In selecting animals for breeding the following points must be considered.

1 Conformity
The animal must conform to the breed type, that is, possess the characteristics of the breed.

2 Performance
The animals must be selected from parents whose performance, for example, milk yield or litter size or food conversion into meat is acceptable.

3 Animal health
Animals selected must be free from diseases, parasites and any form of deformity.

Care and management of animals

In rearing livestock careful consideration must be given to housing, feeding, sanitation, pest and disease control, breeding and the care of young animals.

Housing

Livestock must be protected from the elements. Houses should be constructed of durable materials such as concreted floors, brick walls, well cured hard lumber or steel girders and corrugated metal sheets for covering roofs. The design of the houses depends largely on the type of animal and the management system under which the animal is kept. In constructing houses, the farmer should ensure that there is adequate space for the animal.

Here is a guide to the space requirement (floor area) for some different types of livestock.

Livestock	Space requirement (floor area/animal)
Broilers	30 cm × 30 cm
Layers	1.0 m × 1.0 m
Goat	1.3 m × 1.0 m
Rabbit	1.0 m × 0.6 m
Pregnant Sow	1.6 m × 1.3 m
Pregnant Cow (in a loose box)	3.0 m × 3.0 m

It is essential that the house is well lit, well ventilated and protected from cold air and draughts. The surface of the ground floor should be hard and rough to prevent slipping and there should be proper drainage to facilitate washing and other measures of sanitation. The house should also be provided with adequate watering and feeding devices. Animals such as weaned piglets or kids that are in large numbers or groups are usually kept in community pens.

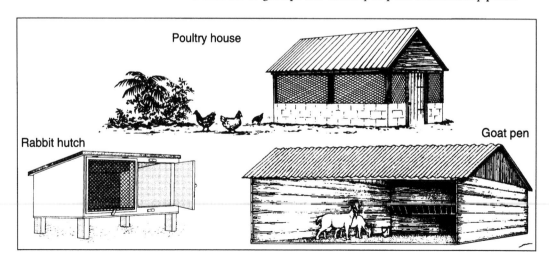

Poultry house

Rabbit hutch

Goat pen

Foods and feeding

Animals feed on a variety of materials such as grasses, legumes, crop residues, hay, silage and manufactured by-products of plant and animal origin. Some of these are coconut meal, citrus pulp meal, soya bean meal, fish meal, bone and meat meal and skimmed milk. There are also a range of specially prepared rations for livestock in different stages of growth and development.

A good ration should contain the essential nutrient elements of carbohydrates, proteins, fats, vitamins and minerals. It is important that animals be fed well-balanced rations, that is, rations containing the essential food nutrients in the correct proportion to suit the purposes for which the animals are reared. Young animals need rations that are high in protein and minerals. Such rations will promote body growth and the development of bones and teeth. For animals in production the ration should take care of the maintenance and production needs of the animal.

Pest and disease control

Animals are exposed to attacks from several types of pests and diseases. The major pests are external parasites like lice, ticks and mites and internal parasites like tape worms and round worms. These parasites cause irritation and uneasiness. They suck the blood of the animals making them anaemic and **unthrifty**. Some of them also spread diseases: the tick spreads the disease organism which causes tick fever in cattle.

Round worm

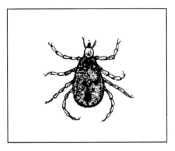

Tick

Diseases are generally caused by micro-organisms such as viruses, bacteria and protozoa. New Castle disease in poultry and rabies in cattle are caused by viruses, whilst diarrhoea and mastitis in goats are caused by bacteria. *Coccidiosis* in poultry and rabbits is caused by a protozoan. These disease organisms are usually spread by the feed and water the animal **ingests** or by contact with the faeces of diseased animals.

Livestock should be protected from these pests and diseases. Preventative measures include the selection of disease-free animals, good sanitation, regular immunisation, the isolation of infected animals and the controlled movement of animals and people in and out of the farm. In the case of infected animals the control measures used are innoculations, injections and the use of medications.

Breeding

Breeding is the act of mating male and female animals to produce offspring, that is, young animals. Breeding is usually done naturally or artificially by insemination as in cattle. Whatever the method of breeding used, the following management factors should be considered.

1 Suitable breeds or types of animals should be selected for breeding. This will depend upon the purpose for which the animal is reared.
2 The animal should be healthy and free from diseases.
3 The animal should be physically fit and ready for mating.
4 Proper records should be kept on the animals reared.

Care of young animals

In our first book you learnt about brooding chicks. Let us now look at some general principles relating to the care and management of young animals.

Care at birth

At birth the young animal should be properly cleaned and dried. The navel or umbilical cord should be cut and painted with iodine.

The young animal should be encouraged to nurse so that it can get the colostrum, that is, the first milk, which is very rich in proteins. This milk also contains antibodies which give the young animal resistance and protection against diseases.

A goat suckling

Housing

The animal should be properly housed. It may be kept with its mother for a period of time and then removed to its own pen. The house should be covered, well lit and ventilated, and provided with heat. The construction of guard rails is often necessary, particularly for pigs, to protect the young animals from getting crushed by the mother.

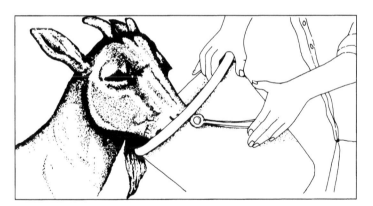

Feeding and watering

In the early stages the animal should be fed on whole milk or milk substitutes. Rations and succulent grasses should be introduced gradually. Pure fresh water should be available at all times.

Control of pests and diseases

The animal should be vaccinated against diseases. In addition good sanitation should be practised. The animal house should be cleaned, washed and disinfected regularly and the utensils for feeding and watering should be properly

Weaning piglets

cleaned before placing new feed and water in them. Deworming the animal to remove intestinal worms and dusting against external parasites may also be necessary.

Weaning of young animals

Weaning is the act of removing young animals from their mothers so that they can feed on their own. This must be done at the stage when the animal is strong enough and is able to feed for itself. Weaning should be gradual so that the young animal will not feel the stress of separation.

Record keeping

Careful records must be kept on both the young animals and the parent. These should show parentage, date of birth, weight at birth, litter size, date and type of vaccinations, feeding data, periodic weight checks and time of weaning. How can these records help the farmer?

The economic importance of livestock

You will remember that a livestock farmer depends upon the sales of his livestock and livestock products to obtain his income. For example, a dairy farmer obtains his income from the sales of his cattle or from the sale of fresh milk to the groceries and dairies. Excess or unsold milk is processed into powdered milk, butter and cheese. These products are traded in foreign markets to bring in **foreign exchange**.

On large farms, the livestock farmer hires labour and so provides employment opportunities for other people. Now explain the economic importance of rearing poultry and pigs.

Summary

Livestock farmers depend upon the sales of their livestock and livestock products for their incomes. The main types of animals reared on livestock farms in the Caribbean are cattle, pigs, goats, sheep, poultry birds and rabbits.

The level of a farmer's income is generally determined by the yield and the quality of products coming from the farm. These two factors are influenced by the proper selection of animals and the type of care and management that the animals get.

In selecting animals, the farmer should consider the purpose for which the animal is reared and the most suitable breed or type of animal for the required purpose or function. For example, dairy cattle are reared mainly for milk, whilst beef cattle are reared for meat. Similarly in poultry, layers are reared for eggs and broilers for meat.

Animals for breeding should be selected with care. They should conform to their breed type and must come from proven parents whose performance is acceptable. The selected animals must be physically fit, healthy and free from diseases, parasitic infection, and deformity.

Very often animals are cross-bred. This is done to improve certain characteristics such as milk yield, growth rate, feed conversion and litter size in the offspring.

In the care and management of livestock, the farmer should ensure that the animals are properly housed and adequately fed. Good sanitation should be maintained in order to protect the animals from pests and diseases and to keep them healthy. The animals should be dewormed periodically.

Young animals need special care and attention. At birth they should be cleaned, dried and the umbilical cord cut and treated. The new born should be encouraged to nurse so as to get the colostrum or first milk. By the second or third week they should be introduced to rations and herbage materials. Water should be provided at all times. It is essential to maintain good sanitation and to protect the animals from pests and diseases.

Weaning should be a gradual process. It is done when the animal is able to feed and stand on its own.

Records are very important. They should show useful information and data so that the farmer can use these for future reference and as a guide.

The livestock industry is economically important. It brings an income to the farmer and provides opportunities for work for other people. The processed products are traded with other countries to bring in foreign exchange.

Remember these

Breeding	Mating male and female animals to produce offspring.
Broilers	Poultry birds reared for meat.
Commercial	For business purposes.
Cross breeding	Mating animals belonging to two different breeds.
Foreign exchange	Money derived from trade with foreign countries.
Income	Money obtained from wages or from the profits of a business enterprise.

Ingest	To eat or take in by the mouth.
Layers	Poultry birds reared for eggs.
Livestock	Animals that are domesticated and reared by farmers.
Unthrifty	Losing body weight resulting from an attack by diseases or by intestinal parasites.

Practical activities

1 Visit a nearby livestock farm and make a list of the animals reared on the farm.
2 Collect and label samples of the following:
  a Herbage materials fed to animals.
  b Rations used as feed.
3 Prepare a picture book showing different breeds of cattle, pig, goat, sheep, poultry bird and rabbit.
4 Observe a poultry or rabbit house. List the materials and state how they are used in the construction of the house.
5 Look at a pig farmer at work on a morning. List his activities in the order in which he performs them.

Do these tests

1 Select the best answer from the choices given.
  a The Leghorn is a breed of
    A cattle
    B pig
    C poultry bird
    D goat
  b A breed of animals refers to animals that
    A belong to the same litter
    B possess similar features or characteristics
    C are bred and reared on the same farm
    D are ready for mating
  c An animal was allocated a floor area of 30 cm × 30 cm. Such an area is most suitable for rearing a
    A broiler bird
    B layer bird
    C rabbit
    D goat
  d The most suitable ration for a young animal is one that is rich in
    A fats and minerals
    B fats and protein
    C carbohydrates and fats
    D proteins and minerals
  e An example of an internal parasite is the
    A louse
    B mite
    C tape-worm
    D tick

2 Name two breeds of
  a dairy cattle
  b dairy goat
  c meat rabbit

3 Name three types of animals reared for work.

4 Explain how the offspring of a Zebu-Holstein cross is likely to differ from either of its parents.

5 List the points that should be considered in selecting animals for breeding.

6 Give three examples of manufactured by-products used as feed and derived from
  a plant origin
  b animal origin

7 Name two diseases in animals caused by
  a a virus
  b a bacterium

8 Say why
  a animals are dewormed
  b young animals must be fed colostrum
  c weaning should be a gradual process

9 Describe how a goat farmer should attend to a kid at birth.

10 State the economic importance of livestock production in agriculture.

12 Rearing rabbits

Lesson objectives

The rabbit is a good source of meat. The meat is soft, delicious and rich in protein. Rabbit pelts are also used in the manufacture of small items. On completing this lesson you should be able to

1 state the purposes for which rabbits are reared.

2 identify the body parts of a rabbit.

3 name a few breeds of rabbits and state the purposes for which they are reared.

4 list the equipment required for rearing rabbits.

5 demonstrate how to handle a rabbit.

6 care for and manage rabbits.

7 identify does that are ready for mating.

8 list some ailments and diseases which affect rabbits.

9 state some precautionary measures that should be taken to prevent and control ailments and diseases in rabbits.

10 draw a rabbit and label the body parts.

You remember that the rabbit is a small animal and is classified as a mammal. It also belongs to the group of animals called rodents. **Rodents** are identified quite easily. They have long, sharp curved incisors, or front teeth, which are specially adapted for gnawing. They are nocturnal animals; this means that they feed and move about more actively at night than by day. Under natural conditions they burrow and live in the ground.

Rabbits in agriculture

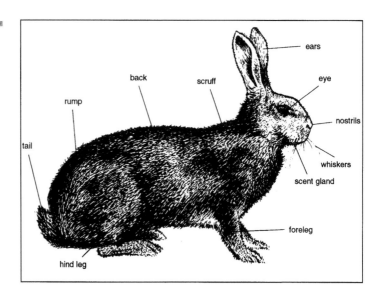

Rabbits are wild in their natural state. They may become a serious pest to the farmer, as they destroy cultivated crops. Many people in the Caribbean rear rabbits as pets. However, rabbit meat is quite good for the table. It is soft, delicious, and a good source of protein. Rabbits grow rapidly and can reach a weight of 1.5 kg to 2 kg in eight weeks. More people should look to the rabbit as their future source of meat supply. Rabbit **pelts**, (their preserved skins with the fur on) are used in the manufacture of small items like purses, bedroom slippers, table mats and hand bags. The sale of live rabbits could also be a profitable concern.

Rabbit breeds

The New Zealand White is a good meat breed

Rabbits are classified according to their uses.

Meat breeds

These rabbits are specially reared for meat. They should be well fleshed and should attain maturity at an early age of eight to ten weeks. The *Flemish Giant, Belgian Hare* and *New Zealand White* are all good meat breeds.

Fur rabbits

The fur rabbits are reared for their pelts. All breeds of rabbits could give pelts, but better quality pelts are obtained from the *Chinchilla* and *Sable* breeds. Their hairs are fine, silky and glossy and are of two definite lengths, with short under-coat hairs and longer guard hairs.

(above) Dutch rabbit;
(middle right) Orange Rex;
(far right) Angora

Wool types

Wool is hair that is fine and wavy in nature. A fine silky wool is obtained from the Angora rabbit.

Other rabbits

There are several other 'fancy' rabbits that are reared for shows and exhibitions. In addition, small rabbits are used extensively in laboratories and experimental programmes.

There are not many rabbit breeds in the Caribbean. It is best to choose breeds that are best adapted to local conditions, and those that are dual-purpose in nature, giving both good meat and pelts.

The *Flemish Giant* and the *New Zealand Whites* seem to thrive best under local conditions. At maturity the *Flemish Giants* attain a weight of 5–7 kg, whilst the *New Zealand Whites* reach a weight of 3.5–5.5 kg.

Housing and equipment

Housing

Rabbits are domesticated and reared in **hutches**. A number of hutches are kept in a rabbitry or rabbit house. Can you give three reasons why rabbits are housed?

The best place to locate a rabbitry is on a flat well-drained area with shady trees around. Trees are specially helpful during hot weather conditions.

Equipment

Hutches

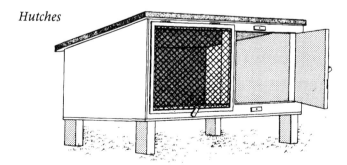

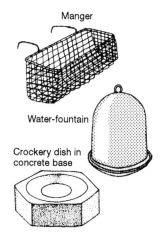

Manger

Water-fountain

Crockery dish in
concrete base

Feed storage bin

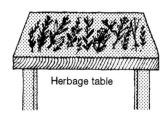

Herbage table

Rabbits are kept in hutches. **Bucks** and pregnant **does** are kept in separate hutches, whilst weaners could be kept as a group in **community pens**.

Hutches are constructed from wood, metal and wire netting. They should have doors and dropping trays.

Feeders, waterers and mangers
Metal or crockery dishes are fixed in concrete bases so that they are not easily tipped over. A manger for **herbage** is also necessary.

Feed bins
Dry feeds and concentrates must be stored in covered bins in order to protect them from pests. Uncovered feeds may become mouldy in damp conditions.

The herbage table
Green succulent feeding material must be stacked on a herbage table. Such material should be collected ten to fifteen hours in advance, properly washed and allowed to wilt before it is fed to the rabbits. Wilting reduces the moisture content of the herbage and this prevents diarrhoea, also known as 'scouring'.

Water source
A water tap is necessary for supplying clean, fresh water. The hutches and the floor of the rabbitry should be washed and cleaned regularly.

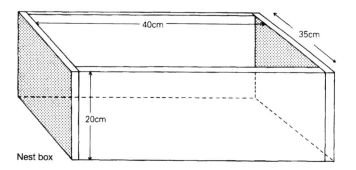

40cm

35cm

20cm

Nest box

Nest boxes
Breeding hutches must be provided with nest boxes. The boxes should be designed to accommodate the doe and the litter, and to facilitate easy cleaning.

Care and management of rabbits

Feeding

Rabbits, like other farm animals, need food for healthy growth and development. A good ration consists of green feeds and concentrates, as well as household scraps.

Green feeds

Green feeds are rich in proteins, vitamins and minerals. Only succulent material should be fed to the animals. Do you know why? It is because the rabbit has a simple stomach and cannot deal with fibrous matter.

Green feeds consist of rabbit meats, patchoi, cabbage, spinach, cauliflower leaves, lettuce, sweet-potato slips, hibiscus leaves and various types of vines. Rabbits also delight in carrots, radish and sweet-potato tubers.

Herbage should be placed in a manger to prevent it from becoming contaminated with the animals' droppings.

Commercial feeds

Commercial feeds for rabbits are not readily obtained in local markets. However, chick starter rations or broiler starter rations are good substitutes. Rations are needed to supplement green feeds, and just enough should be given so that the animal can eat it in twenty minutes. Pregnant mothers and does with litters should be given additional rations. Baby rabbits should consume about 56 g to 70 g of feed daily by weaning time, that is, when they are seven to eight weeks old.

Household scraps

Rabbits accept fresh kitchen scraps, such as crusts, and fresh milk. Meat and greasy foods should be avoided.

Water

A supply of pure, fresh water must be maintained regularly in the hutch. Rabbits drink a lot of water and it is especially important that a doe with a litter has a steady supply.

Mineral licks

Mineral licks are blocks of salts of calcium, magnesium, phosphorus and other minerals. Small blocks of mineral salts should be placed in the hutch periodically so as to provide the minerals the animals need to build bones and teeth.

Frequency of feeding

How often should rabbits be fed? Twice a day seems quite adequate, that is, once in the morning and once in the afternoon. Since the rabbits are more active at night they should be given a heavier meal in the afternoon.

Handling rabbits

A rabbit must be held or lifted with care. The loose skin on the shoulder or scruff should be grasped by the left hand and the hindquarters or rump supported by the right hand.

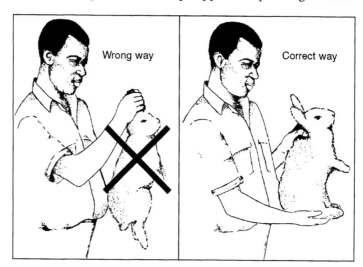

Wrong way

Correct way

A rabbit should never be held by its ears as this causes injury. A cage should be used if the animal is to be transported long distances.

Sanitation

Dirty hutches, dirty feed and water utensils, and mouldy feeds lead to infection and disease. The entire rabbitry must be kept absolutely clean. Leftovers and animal droppings should be removed daily. Utensils should be cleaned before serving new meals, whilst the entire rabbitry should be washed and disinfected every eight to ten days.

Mating of rabbits

Breeding age

The breeding age of rabbits varies with different breeds. *New Zealand Whites* and *Flemish Giants* can be bred at the age of eight to ten months. However, it is important that the animal be physically matured before first mating.

Mating time

Does are ready for mating when they:

(a) are restless and nervous.

(b) make efforts to join rabbits in other hutches.

(c) rub their chins on mangers and water containers.
(d) scratch the floor with their fore and hind legs.

The mating of does

Does are taken to the buck for mating when they will readily accept service. After mating the doe is taken back to her hutch. By the end of a month (31 days) she should be ready for **kindling**.

Pregnancy

The **pregnancy** period in rabbits is thirty-one (31) days. During this time the pregnant does are kept by themselves and are given special care. They should not be excited or handled too often. The hutches should be opened only at regular feeding and watering time. Proper feeding and sanitation should be maintained.

Kindling

At kindling time the doe begins making her nest, which may be two to eight days before kindling. A nestbox with straw should be placed in the hutch just before the doe begins to make her nest. Notice how she pulls the fur off her body. There should be no disturbance during kindling.

Baby rabbits, also called kittens, are born in **litters** with the size of the litter varying from one kindling to another. The kittens are usually born naked, that is, without hair on them. Their eyes are fully opened when they are about sixteen days old and they move and begin to feed with their mothers by the eighteenth day.

Weaning

The young rabbits are weaned when they are seven to eight weeks old. Soon after, the doe shows signs of being ready for mating. When this occurs, she should be taken to the buck for service.

The prevention and treatment of diseases

Rabbits thrive well under good systems of feeding and management. However, there are some common ailments and diseases that may lead to death.

Snuffles

A rabbits suffering from snuffles appears to have a bad cold with a running nose. It rubs its nose with its fore-paws. Any rabbit with snuffles should be removed and put into a warm place free from draughts. The application of a drop of Eucalyptus oil to each nostril would help.

Coccidiosis

This is a protozoan disease. Rabbits become droopy and lose appetite and weight. The disease can be controlled by the use of sulphur drugs. It is advisable to destroy all animals suspected of carrying the disease. Good sanitation and management are absolutely vital. The animals should be well fed, their hutches should be scrubbed and disinfected, the feed and water containers properly cleaned, and the entire rabbitry washed and sprayed before introducing any new stock.

Bloat

The animal appears to be swollen, and there may also be some scouring. The disease may be caused by stomach upsets due to mouldy feeds or improperly balanced rations.

The animal should be removed to a sick bay. Only dry feeds should be given for a day or two.

Internal parasites

Rabbits may be infested with internal parasites such as tape-worms, round worms and *coccidia*. These cause scouring and thriftlessness. These parasites are best controlled by sanitation and good management practices.

Sore hocks

Some rabbits are tender and could suffer damage of the hind legs on rough or wire-netted floors. The hock should be washed with an antiseptic, treated with a healing ointment, and the rabbit placed on a soft, smooth floor.

Summary

The rabbit is a mammal belonging to a group of animals called rodents. It is a nocturnal animal which moves and feeds more actively by night than by day. Under natural conditions it burrows and lives in the ground.

Rabbits are often reared as pets. However, they are a good source of meat and their pelts are used in the manufacture of small items such as purses, tablemats and bedroom slippers.

There are several breeds of rabbits. The *Flemish Giant*, the *Belgian Hares* and the *New Zealand White* are reared for meat whilst the *Chinchilla* and the *Sable* breeds are reared mainly for pelts. There are also some breeds reared for exhibitions and shows.

Rabbits are usually kept in hutches in a rabbitry, that is, a rabbit house. The hutches are provided with feed trays, water containers and mangers for holding succulent green feeds. The animals are fed on rations along with wilted herbage materials. Pure fresh water is always available.

Proper sanitation is an essential requirement. Feed trays and water containers should be washed before a new meal is given and the droppings and remains of herbage materials removed. The floor of the rabbit house should be washed and disinfected daily.

Great care should be taken when handling rabbits. The scruff should be grasped by the left hand and the hindquarters supported by the right. This is necessary because the rabbit is a delicate animal.

During pregnancy, the doe is kept by herself in a breeding hutch containing a nest box. The animal should not be excited or handled too often. Two to eight days before kindling time the doe begins to make a nest by pulling the fur from its body. When the baby rabbits or kittens are born, they are usually naked and blind. Within three weeks their eyes are fully opened and they begin to move around with their mothers. They are weaned when they are seven to eight weeks old.

The most common ailments and diseases affecting rabbits are snuffles, coccidiosis, bloat, internal parasites and sore hocks. These, however, could be kept under control by good systems of feeding and management.

Remember these

Buck	A male rabbit.
Community pen	A pen in which a group of animals are kept.
Doe	A female rabbit.
Herbage	Soft plants and grasses.
Hutch	Accommodation made from wood and mesh in which rabbits are kept.
Kindling	Giving birth to young rabbits.
Litter	A number of young animals born at the same time.
Pelts	The cured coat of the rabbit consisting of the skin with fur or hair attached.
Pregnancy	The period during which an animal is in young.
Rodents	A group of mammals identified by their long sharp curved incisors adapted for gnawing.

Practical activities

1 a Observe a live rabbit and identify the parts of its body.
  b Make a drawing of a rabbit and label its body parts.
2 Collect a handful of mature para grass and a head of patchoi. Allow them to wilt and then feed to rabbits. Which of the two feed materials was better accepted by the animals? Give reasons for your observations.
3 Collect the necessary materials and construct a nest box of the same dimensions given in this lesson.
4 Observe a litter of rabbits from kindling time to one month of age. Find answers for the following.
  a How many baby rabbits are born in the litter?
  b Are their eyes open or are they born blind?
  c Are they covered with hair or are they naked?
  d How long after birth are their eyes fully opened?
  e When do they begin to move about and feed?
5 Demonstrate to your classmates how to handle a rabbit. Remember to grasp the scruff by the left hand and support the hind quarters or rump by the right hand.
6 Select and weigh a rabbit at weaning time. Weigh the same rabbit at weekly intervals for four weeks after weaning. Ensure that the animal is given adequate care and management.

Complete the table by recording the weights obtained.

Weighing intervals	Weight of animal in kg
Weight at weaning time	
Weight one week later	
Weight two weeks later	
Weight three weeks later	
Weight four weeks later	

a Comment on weight gained or lost.

b Give reasons for differences observed.

Do these test exercises

1 Complete the following sentences by filling the blank spaces with the correct words or phrases selected from the brackets at the end of the sentences.

a The rabbit is called a mammal because (it is cold blooded, it can run and jump, it suckles its young).

b Pelts are .... (preserved rabbit skins with the fur on, preserved rabbit skins without the fur).

c The angora breed of rabbit is noted for its .... (wool, fur, meat).

d The gestation period of a rabbit is .... (21 days, 31 days, 35 days).

e A litter of rabbits is .... (a group of six rabbits, a number of young animals born at the same time, young animals born from different parents).

2 Select the best answer from the choices given.

a The rabbit is described as a nocturnal animal because it is

A a very active animal.

B not active at all.

C more active by day than by night.

D more active by night than by day.

b Which of the following rabbits is NOT reared for meat production?

A Angora

B Flemish Giant

C Belgian Hare

D New Zealand White

c A doe scratches the floor of the hutch with her fore and hind legs. This indicates that she is

A very hungry

B ready for mating

C about to kindle

D suffering from snuffles

d Kindling is the act of

A keeping young rabbits warm

B a mother nursing baby rabbits

C giving birth to young rabbits

D mating a doe for the first time

e To wean an animal is to

A remove it from one hutch to another

B separate it from its mother

C allow it to move and feed with its mother

D place the baby rabbit in a community pen

3 Say why the following is done in rabbit keeping:

a Succulent materials are allowed to wilt before they are fed to the rabbits.

b Mineral licks are placed in the rabbit hutch.

c Carriers or suspects are destroyed.

d A rabbit is given its heavier meal in the afternoon.

4 Give answers to the following.

a A rabbit ready for mating shows what signs?

b What are the causes of bloat?

c For what reasons are young animals weaned?

d List four ways in which sanitation in rearing rabbits is maintained.

5 Your teacher assigns you to take care of the rabbits in school during the morning shift. Write an account of all the operations you would perform in attending to your rabbits.

13

Rearing goats and sheep

Lesson objectives

Goats and sheep are found throughout the Caribbean. These animals are classified as small livestock, and can be reared by the poorest farmer as they are not expensive and do not need costly housing or large areas of grazing land. On completing this lesson you should be able to:

1 Name the products obtained from goats and sheep.

2 Identify some breeds of goats and sheep.

3 List the features associated with a few breeds of goats and sheep.

4 Identify the body parts of goats and sheep.

5 State the points that should be considered in selecting goats and sheep for breeding.

6 Describe the systems of management under which goats and sheep are reared.

7 Describe the care and management of does and ewes during pregnancy.

8 Describe the care and management of breeding bucks and rams.

9 Describe the care and management of kids and lambs from birth to weaning time.

10 Identify some fodder grasses and rations suitable as feeds for goats and sheep.

11 Describe the process of digestion in the ruminant stomach.

12 List some common pests and diseases of goats and sheep.

13 State some preventative and control measures of pest and diseases in goats and sheep.

Goats and sheep are reared in many of the Caribbean islands.

Look at this herd of goats. Notice how they browse on the shrubs, and graze on the grass which grows on the hillside. They feed on poor scrubby plants and convert them into valuable animal products.

Goats and sheep supply us with meat, milk, wool, hair, and hides. In some countries the hair of the Angora goat is used for making carpets, bags and ropes. Farmers use the manure from goat and sheep pens to enrich their garden soils so that they can grow better crops.

Goats and sheep thrive best under dry conditions. However, in the wetter parts of the Caribbean they are reared successfully on the hillsides or on light sandy soils. Very wet conditions may cause the animals to suffer from pneumonia and hoof-rot disease.

Breeds of goat and sheep

Goats vary in their size and weight and in their ability to give milk. Some of them may be polled (hornless) while others may have wattles. Sheep are reared throughout the region, although not as many as goats. The types found in the Caribbean are prolific. The young animals grow and develop quickly and are ready for the market at ten to twelve months old.

Goats and sheep are classified as small livestock. They are similar in their body structure. The diagram on this page will help you to recognise the different parts of the animal.

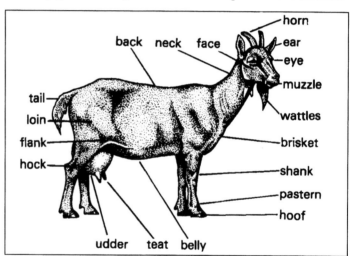

There are several breeds of goat. The *British Alpine* and the *Saanen* are noted for their milk production, whilst the *Anglo-Nubians* are dual-purpose – that is, they are both meat and milk producers. The *Angora* goat is reared chiefly for skins and hides. However, it is not commonly found in the Caribbean. The local dwarf goat is made up of several crosses, and is specially adapted for meat production.

Among the breeds of sheep reared in the region, the *Barbados Black Belly* sheep is the most promising. Experimental work is also done on the *Blackhead Persian* to determine whether it is adaptable to Caribbean conditions.

Let us look more closely at some of these breeds of goats and sheep that are reared in the Caribbean and neighbouring countries.

Dairy goats

British Alpine goat

British Alpine

This goat originated in the Swiss and Austrian Alps. It is black and white in colour and is a quiet, docile animal. It thrives reasonably well under wet, humid conditions and gives as much as 4–4.5 kg of milk a day.

Saanen

The Saanen is Swiss in origin. It is white to cream in colour, with black spots on the nose, ears, and udder. It has a short coat, erect ears, and is generally **polled**, or hornless.

The Saanen thrives best on cool hillsides as it is very sensitive to light and hot weather conditions. Under favourable conditions it gives as much as 4–4.5 kg of milk per day.

Dual-purpose goats

Anglo-Nubian

The Anglo-Nubian is of mixed origin. It is a cross between an English goat and a good Indian milker. It has long legs, a convex facial line, lop ears, and is usually polled. This goat is hardy, well fleshed, and gives from 3.5–4 kg of milk a day. The Anglo-Nubian performs well under local conditions. It appears to be the animal best suited for the Caribbean and surrounding regions.

Dwarf goats (meat type)

The local dwarf goats are reared exclusively for meat. They have short legs and grow to a weight of 18–20 kg. Their growth rate is slow, and their milk yields are low. These goats thrive quite well under wet, humid conditions.

Try to identify the breeds of goat reared in your school or in your village area. Which breed or type is found in the greatest number?

Other breeds of goats

The *Toggenburg* and the *Jumnapari* are good dairy goats. These are not reared on a large scale, but are used mainly in breeding programmes to upgrade milk production of local stocks.

Breeds of sheep

Barbados Black Belly

The Barbados Black belly sheep was bred in the island of Barbados. It has a hairy coat, brown in colour with black under the belly. The tail is of medium length and both ewes and rams are polled.

This sheep can withstand the **heat stress** of tropical conditions and can breed at any time of the year. It is very **prolific** and generally produces twins or triplets at birth. The animal is ready for slaughtering at the age of ten months to a year when it attains a weight of 33 to 35 kilograms. The meat is firm and not very fatty.

Blackhead Persian

The Blackhead Persian is a breed of Central and South American sheep reared for meat. As the name implies, its head is black and the rest of its body is white in colour. The ram as well as the ewe is polled. It is used in cross breeding programmes to improve the **carcase** quality, that is, the meat quality, in local stock.

Other breeds and crosses are found in the region, but they are of no great significance in livestock production.

Selection, breeding and reproduction

Goats and sheep that are to be used as breeding animals should be selected from strong, healthy, high-yielding parents. Such animals must conform to their breed types and show good growth rates. They should be docile, alert, and bright in appearance, and their skin should be soft and fine. Animals intended for dairy purposes should have large soft udders with well formed teats, well developed chests, a deep barrel or abdominal cavity and a wedge-shaped body. Their milk yields should be high.

The selection of male and female animals (bucks and does/rams and ewes) may begin at weaning time, which is three to four months after birth.

However, the final selection should be made when the animals are six or seven months old.

Mating should not take place until the animals are mature or physically developed. For most does or ewes this occurs when they are eleven to twelve months old.

A doe or ewe is ready for mating when she is on oestrus or heat. At this stage she is often restless, her vulva is flushed and swollen, she swishes her tail profusely and allows herself to be mounted by other members in the herd. When this is observed, the doe or ewe should be taken to the male for service after which she is returned to her own pen.

In goats, oestrus lasts for 24 to 36 hours and the oestrous cycle takes place every 18–21 days. In sheep these periods are slightly shorter. Oestrus lasts for 12–24 hours and the oestrous cycle takes place every 16–18 days.

Care and management of does and ewes during pregnancy

Pregnancy is the period from conception to the time the doe or ewe gives birth to her young. This period is also known as the **gestation** period and lasts for approximately 150 to 152 days in goats. In sheep it is 145 to 147 days.

During pregnancy the doe or ewe needs special care and attention because she has to take care of herself and her young. She must have free access to pastures and adequate supplies of water, feeds and mineral licks. Remember that mineral licks are important as they are needed for building the body and bones of the developing foetus.

A week before delivery the pregnant mother should be brought to the kidding or lambing pen. This will protect her from the weather and will enable the farmer to assist and take care of the mother and her young when delivery takes place.

Goat with kid

Care and management of breeding bucks or rams

A buck or ram is ready to serve when he is twelve to fourteen months old. He may be allowed to run in the pastures with the rest of the herd, but it is better to keep him separately and to bring the doe or ewe to him for service when she is ready. The farmer is then able to keep careful records of services, pregnancies, and the performance of the animals. The buck or ram should also be provided with adequate shelter, feed, pasture and water supply.

Management, housing and care

Systems of management

Goats or sheep may be reared intensively or extensively. An intensive system caters for a large population of animals that are reared within a limited space. The animals must be properly housed, well fed and watered, and there must be adequate sanitation and protection from pests and diseases. This system is suited to dairy animals as they need much care and attention.

The extensive system of management is better suited for meat-producing animals. The animals are given little protection from the environment, and a minimum of labour and management is involved.

The animals graze freely in the open pastures. There is no fencing or housing, and they are herded only when they are needed. However, the farmer must ensure that the climatic conditions are favourable, pastures are adequate, and water is available. Shade trees are desirable in the pastures as the animals are small and suffer from heat stress. Do you know the effect of heat stress on animals? The animals tend to eat less and they drink large quantities of water. There is a loss of energy and body weight and a decrease in growth.

Many farmers prefer to rear their animals in a semi-intensive system – the animals are housed at night and put on pastures during the day. Why is this system of management used in many of our countries?

Housing and equipment

Goats are very small animals and they do not need very elaborate housing. However, the houses must be covered, well-ventilated, provided with feeding rack, watering devices, and facilities for rations and mineral licks. For dairy goats a milking stand may be necessary. Measures for cleaning and sanitation should also be taken into consideration. The pictures on the following page show you some simple types of goat housing and equipment.

Foods and feeding

Look at your goat or sheep as it feeds in the pasture. Notice how it moves its upper lip and uses its tongue to gather the leaves and shoots from the surrounding plants. The animal is an inquisitive and selective feeder and wanders for great distances, browsing on all materials that it reaches to neck height.

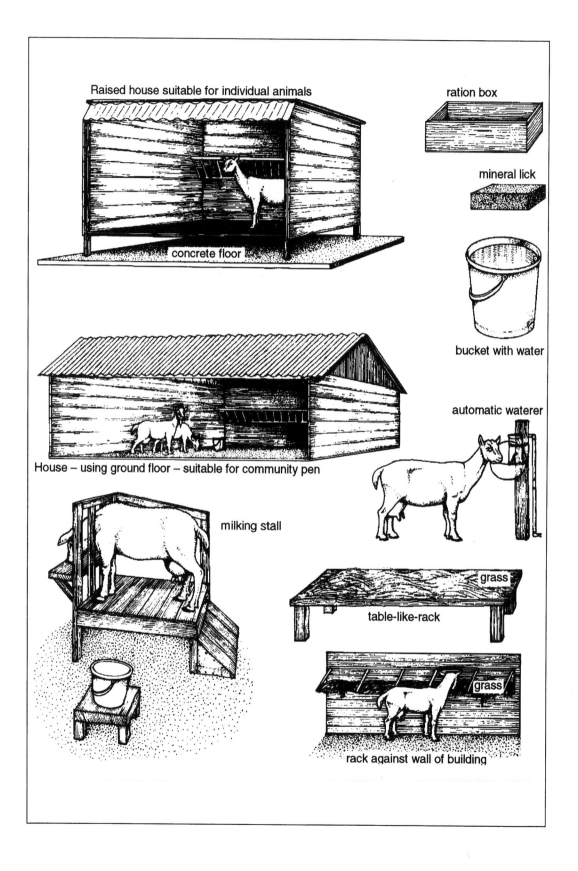

Raised house suitable for individual animals

ration box

concrete floor

mineral lick

bucket with water

House – using ground floor – suitable for community pen

automatic waterer

milking stall

grass

table-like-rack

grass

rack against wall of building

Goats and sheep require adequate quantities of carbo-hydrates, fats, proteins, vitamins, mineral salts, and water in their diets. These nutrients are obtained from pastures and fodder grasses, commercial feeds, and mineral licks.

Pasture and fodder grasses as feeds
Goats and sheep are **ruminants**. This means that they chew their cud. Ruminants have large, complex stomachs and the bulk of their food consists of plant material. The animals will readily consume fodder grasses such as elephant, guinea and para grass, or graze on pangola pastures. Remember that pastures should not be over-grazed nor the grasses be allowed to become old and fibrous. **Rotational grazing** helps to maintain regular pastures and control diseases and parasites. Some legumes should be grown in the pasture as these are rich in nitrogen and are important in building body proteins.

The picture on page 154 shows you the complex stomach of ruminants. You will notice that the ruminant's stomach is made up of four compartments: the rumen or paunch; the reticulum or honeycomb, the omasum or manyplies; and the abomasum or true stomach.

The rumen or paunch
The rumen is the largest of the four compartments. Its walls are muscular and it occupies about three quarters of the whole abdominal cavity. Grasses and leaves eaten by the animal are stored in the rumen. During rumination, that is, the chewing of the cud, the food is brought back to the mouth, chewed with saliva, and swallowed again. Further breakdown of cellulose in the rumen takes place by means of bacterial activity. From the rumen, the food materials enter the reticulum (or honeycomb).

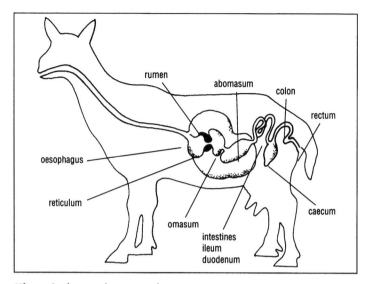

The reticulum or honeycomb

The reticulum is the smallest of the four compartments. The surface is made up of pits and intersecting ridges, and is like a honeycomb in appearance. Foods which enter the reticulum are mixed with liquids, grounded finer, and passed into the omasum.

The omasum or manyplies

The omasum is spherical in shape, that is, like a ball. It is very muscular and is made up of a number of folds or leaves on which there are short horny burr-like structures. Food materials from the reticulum enter between the folds or leaves of the omasum and are ground further. Fluids are

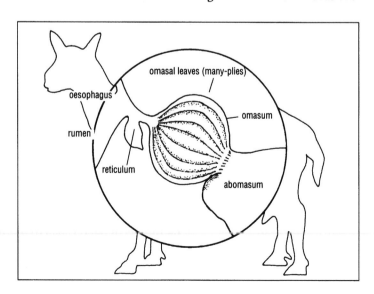

squeezed out and the food is passed on to the abomasum.

The abomasum or true stomach

The abomasum is the true stomach of the goat. Food present here is acted upon chemically by gastric juices secreted by various glands found in the tissues of the stomach. The contents of the abomasum pass into the small and large intestines for further digestion and absorption. The waste substances are passed out as excreta, that is, urine and dung.

Commercial feeds

Commercial feeds or rations are needed for intensively reared meat or dairy goats. These rations should cater for both the maintenance and production requirements of the animal. A **maintenance ration** is the amount of food needed to keep an animal alive and healthy, whereas a **production ration** is the food added so that the animal will put on weight or increase its milk yield.

Rations are made to suit the stage of growth of the animal or the production purposes for which the animal is reared. For example a kid or lamb receives a starter ration, a milking animal gets a lactation ration, whereas a meat animal nearing the stage for slaughter is given a finishing ration. The daily quantity of feed that each animal gets is determined from a feeding chart or guide.

Mineral licks

You will remember that minerals are needed for building bones and teeth. Large quantities of minerals are also present in milk. Goats and sheep need large quantities of calcium, phosphorus, magnesium, and sodium. Grazing animals readily obtain these from the leaves and shoots of plants. Where animals are kept in pens they should be provided with mineral licks.

Water supply

Water is essential for all animals. It is important in the digestion of food and for evaporative cooling. Clean fresh water should always be provided for the animals either in buckets or by means of automatic waterers.

Feeding and sanitation

Goats and sheep are clean feeders. They will not eat trampled grass or drink dirty water. It is important that their pens are cleaned regularly, old rations are removed before new ones are given, buckets properly washed and refilled with fresh water, and fodder grasses hung or placed on a feeding rack.

Grooming

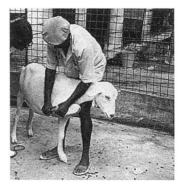

Gentle handling is essential. Coats should be brushed daily and clipped when overgrown. It is also necessary to prune their hoofs periodically, and to give them a dip or a soap-water wash once a month.

Raising kids and lambs

Kidding and lambing time

The pregnant doe or ewe should be brought into the pen a week before delivery time. The floor of the pen must be kept dry and warm with litter or bedding. On the days before and after giving birth the mother should be fed lightly, but she should have free access to water.

At kidding or lambing time there should be no disturbance. After the young animals are born, they should be dried and their navel cords dressed with iodine. The wet or smeared bedding must be removed and replaced with dry bedding. The placenta or afterbirth is dropped a few hours later. This should be removed.

Feeding kids and lambs

Kids and lambs should be suckling within two hours of birth. Sometimes it is necessary to teach them to do so. Remember that all young animals must get the colostrum, that is, the milk produced for the first two or three days after the birth of the kids or lambs. Colostrum is rich in proteins, vitamins and minerals. It stimulates the digestive tracts and builds up immunity against diseases.

For the first few days the kid or lamb is allowed to run with the mother and to suckle freely. In the case of dairy goats, the kids are separated from their mothers when they are a week old. Their feeding is controlled, that is, they are given specific quantities of whole warm milk or milk substitute at particular feeding hours and they are not allowed to drink it too quickly.

When the young animals are about two to three weeks old they should be introduced to starter rations and succulent grasses. This helps to develop the rumen. Clean fresh water and mineral licks should also be provided.

Weaning

Kids and lambs are weaned (separated from their mothers) when they are about eight to ten weeks old. (In the case of dairy goats they could be weaned at one week). By this time they will be grazing and eating about 220 – 230 g of commercial rations daily. They will not need milk substitute. They should then be reared in community pens or put in clean pastures.

Other management practices

Kids and lambs reared under intensive conditions should be provided with an open run for exercise. The males are dehorned during their first week after birth and those males that are not needed for breeding are castrated (that is, their testicles are taken out) when they are seven to nine days old. In lambs, docking, that is, cutting off the tails, might be necessary to reduce fly problems and facilitate mating of the ewes. Sexing is generally done at weaning time.

Intestinal worms can be a severe problem. The young animals are dewormed for the first time when they are about three months old and then periodically every three to four weeks.

Meat and milk products

Goats and sheep convert grasses efficiently into meat and can be slaughtered when they are about seven to ten months old. About 30 per cent of the animal's carcase consists of guts or offal. This means that the amount of dressed meat which can be sold is only about 40 to 45 per

Goat's carcase at a market

cent of the weight of the live animal. However, the meat fetches a high price, especially when it is lean with very little fat.

You will remember that dairy goats are reared for milk. Goats' milk is well suited for babies and invalids. The milk contains small fat globules. It is alkaline in nature, rich in calcium, phosphorus and chlorine and is very easily digested.

Goats' milk tends to have a strong odour. This could be avoided by keeping the bucks away from the milking herds. Hair should not get into the bucket with the milk. The does must be well groomed, their coats kept short, and hygienic conditions must be maintained. Odour is due to the presence of caproic acid secreted by the skin glands of the animal.

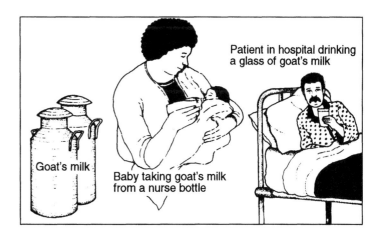

Patient in hospital drinking a glass of goat's milk

Goat's milk

Baby taking goat's milk from a nurse bottle

The prevention and control of pests and diseases

A healthy goat or sheep is always bright, alert and very active. It has a smooth shiny coat, eats well, puts on good body weight and yields plenty of milk.

A healthy goat

Goats and sheep are very hardy animals, but they are still susceptible to certain pests and diseases. In this section of the lesson we will study a few of the common pests and diseases of goats and sheep.

Small dull looking goat with pot belly

Roundworms of the stomach and intestines

This goat is infested with intestinal worms. Several types of roundworm infest the stomach and intestine, of goats and sheep. The large round worm and hair worm live chiefly in the stomach (abomasum) while the nodular worm and the whip worm infest the intestines.

These worms puncture the walls of the stomach and intestines and suck the blood. They irritate the tissues, leaving nodules or swellings behind which affect digestion.

The infected animals become anaemic as a result of a lack of haemoglobin in the blood. They lose their appetite, suffer from diarrhoea (or scours), and lose body weight.

The diagram opposite shows you the life cycle of the large roundworm of the stomach. Study it carefully and find out how a healthy animal gets infected with worms.

These parasitic worms are best prevented by proper management. The animals should be kept well fed – strong, healthy animals develop resistance against worms.

Pastures should be grazed in rotation. Infested pasture should be rested and adverse climatic conditions allowed to kill the infective eggs.

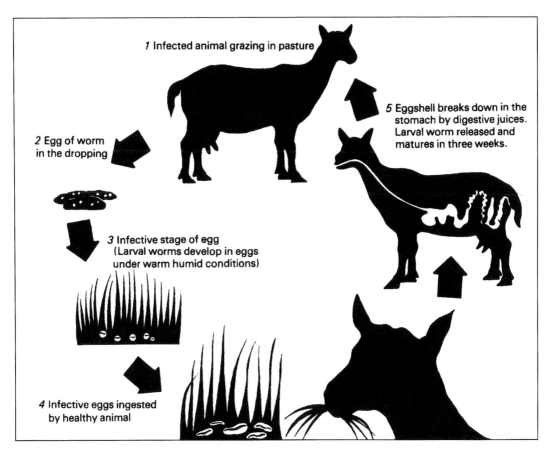

1 Infected animal grazing in pasture

2 Egg of worm in the dropping

3 Infective stage of egg (Larval worms develop in eggs under warm humid conditions)

4 Infective eggs ingested by healthy animal

5 Eggshell breaks down in the stomach by digestive juices. Larval worm released and matures in three weeks.

Young kids and lambs should not be put on the same pastures with older goats and sheep. Animals should be dewormed periodically. Livestock farmers should consult the animal health department of their country for advice on the use of vermicides (chemicals which destroy worms) for their animals.

Lice

Goats and sheep may be infested by sucking lice or by biting lice. The former pierce the skin, suck blood, and leave bumps or sores on the body. Biting lice feed on hair particles or on other foreign objects that may be present on the hair. They move about the surface of the skin and cause irritation.

The diagram on the next page shows you the life cycle of the louse. Note that the eggs are laid on the hairs and hatch out into nymphs in one to three weeks' time. Three weeks later they reach the adult stage, ready to begin the cycle all over again.

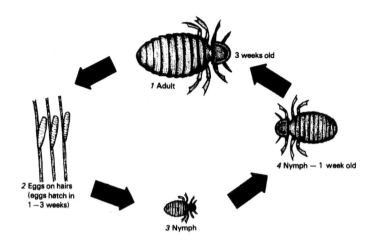

Lice are spread by means of contact. They are readily controlled by isolating infested animals from the herd, clipping their coats short, and by treating them with a dip – that is, by dipping the animals for a short time in a solution of either *Toxaphene* or *Sevin*.

Scabies
Scabies is caused by parasitic mites. The mites puncture the skin and feed on the blood serum (liquid part of the blood) which oozes out. Lesions (sores) develop on the bitten spots, resulting in itching and irritation.

Scabies is spread by means of contact. The parasites are best controlled by the use of dips containing sulphur of lime.

Ticks
Ticks suck the blood of the animals, causing anaemia, and are also responsible for spreading the disease anaplasmosis. Ticks are controlled by spraying or dusting with *Sexin* powder.

Scours (Diarrhoea)
Scours or diarrhoea in goats often results from heavy infestation of the stomach and intestines with harmful bacteria, *coccidia* and worms. These organisms damage the walls of the digestive tract and cause bleeding and digestive disorders. Scours may also take place when the animals eat stale, mouldy food or young, succulent fodder grasses.

The farmer feeds his goats well and ensures that the food is not stale or mouldy and that the fodder grasses are not too young or succulent.

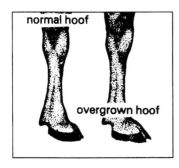

Hoof rot (decaying hoof)

Hoof rot results from bacterial infection. The disease is prevalent among goats that are reared on damp pastures and among animals whose overgrown hoofs are unpared or damaged.

The hoofs of infected animals must first be trimmed and then soaked in a 10 per cent solution of copper sulphate. The treated animals should be kept dry until their hoofs are better.

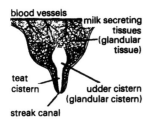

Mastitis

Mastitis is a disease of the udder. It is caused by a bacterium which enters the orifice of the teat and finds its way to the milk-secreting tissues. The bacteria multiply rapidly and destroy the surrounding tissues. Look at this diagram and see how the goat's udder is made up.

An udder infected with mastitis is swollen and tense. It is hard and painful to the touch. The teat is stretched and becomes very red and shiny. The milk is thick with clots. In severe cases of infection the milk may be blood-stained and often has an offensive smell. A goat infected with mastitis suffers a great deal. The body temperature rises, there is a loss of appetite and the animal moves with extreme discomfort.

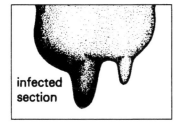

The farmer controls mastitis by keeping his animals clean and by milking them properly. He strips the udder so that no milk is left in it.

When the goats are infected, the farmer massages the udder gently and strips out as much milk as possible. He applies warmth to the udder and inserts an **antibiotic** (a chemical which destroys the bacteria) into the udder through the orifice in the teat.

Summary

Goats and sheep are reared in many of the Caribbean islands. They are not expensive, nor do they need very costly houses or large areas of grazing lands. They supply us with meat, milk, wool, hair and hides.

There are several breeds of goats. The **British Alpine** and the **Saanen** are dairy or milk goats, whilst the **Anglo Nubian** is dual purpose. The dwarf goats are reared mainly for meat.

The sheep that thrives best in the Caribbean region is the *Barbados Black Belly*, and it is reared for meat. The *Blackhead Persian* is also a meat animal but at present it is used experimentally in cross-breeding programmes.

Goats and sheep used as breeding animals should be selected from strong, healthy, high-yielding parents. They should conform to their breed types and show good growth rates. Animals intended for dairy purposes should have large soft udders, well formed teats, well developed chests, and wedge-shaped bodies. The selection of such animals is first done at weaning time and finally when they are about six to seven months old. Does and ewes are mated when they are at the age of eleven to twelve months whereas buck and rams are usually ready to serve when they are about twelve to fourteen months old.

Goats or sheep may be reared intensively, extensively or under semi-intensive conditions. In the Caribbean, livestock farmers prefer the semi-intensive system where the animals are put on pastures during the day and kept in pens at night. Whatever the system of management, the animals should be provided with shelter, feed consisting of rations and forage materials, mineral licks and water supply. The animals should also be groomed regularly.

It must be remembered that goats and sheep are ruminants. They have complex stomachs and are able to digest pasture and fooder grasses quite easily.

Pregnant animals need special care and attention. These should be brought into the pens a week before kidding or lambing time. At the time of delivery the farmer should assist the mothers, clean and dry the young animals, treat their navels and help them to nurse in order to get the colostrum which is essential for them.

Proper records should be made, showing date of birth, number of animals born and the parentage of the animals.

Young animals are fed on whole milk or milk substitutes. They are introduced to starter rations and succulent grasses by the third week. Other care and management practices include sexing, de-horning, castration and worming. In the case of lambs, docking might be necessary. By the third or fourth month after birth, the animals are weaned completely and no longer fed on milk.

Goats and sheep are attacked by several pests and

diseases. Roundworms and hair worms puncture the stomach walls and suck the blood of the animals whilst lice, mites and ticks cause loss of blood, irritation and skin injury, and even spread diseases. A rotational grazing plan and medications should be used as prevention and control measures against these parasites.

Other problems likely to occur are scours, hoof rot and mastitis. Proper feeding, sanitation, and good pasture management and milking practices should be adopted in the control of these problems.

Remember these

Antibiotic	A chemical which destroys bacterial organisms.
Carcase	The body of an animal that has been slaughtered for meat.
Gestation	The period during which an animal is in young.
Heat stress	The harmful effects of high temperatures on feeding, water consumption, body weight and growth of animals.
Maintenance ration	The amount of food required to keep an animal alive and healthy.
Polled animals	Animals without horns.
Production ration	The extra feed given to an animal so that it will put on fat or increase its milk yield.
Prolific	Very productive.
Rotational grazing	A planned system of grazing in which the animals are rotated from one section of a pasture to another.
Ruminants	Animals with complex stomachs which allow them to eat and digest fibrous foods.

Practical Activities

1 Observe a goat or sheep and identify its body parts

2 Visit a farm on which goats and sheep are reared. Make invesitgations on the animals and use the information to complete the table below.

Animals	Breeds	Purpose for which it is reared	Descriptions of the animal
Goats			
Sheep			

3 Make a diagram of the complex stomach of a goat or sheep and label the parts.

4 Collect and label specimens of the following:

a Goat and sheep products.

b Rations and fodder grasses fed to goats and sheep.

c Parasites found in goats and sheep.

5 A goat or sheep gave birth to young. Complete the records below.

Date of birth	Litter size	Sex		Birth Weight	Parentage		Date of Weaning
		No. of Male	No. of Female		Sire	Dam	

How can this information help a livestock farmer?

1 Select the best answer from the choices given.

a A good dual-purpose goat is the

A British Alpine

B Saanen

C Anglo-Nubian

D Dwarf goat

b Which of the following is a breed of sheep?

A Toggenberg

B Blackhead Persian

C Jumnapari

D Angora

c The oestrous cycle in sheep takes place every

A 14 to 15 days

B 16 to 18 days

C 19 to 21 days

D 22 to 23 days

d A livestock farmer bought lactation rations for his animals. It is likely that the animals were

A recently weaned

B in their early pregnancy

C about to be slaughtered

D in milk production

e Some goats developed dull, ruffled coats, pot bellies and lost body weight. These goats were suffering from

A intestinal worms

B scours

C scabies

D mastitis

2 Explain in your own words:

a the effect that heat-stress has on goats and sheep.

b how milk odours can be avoided

c why kids should not be put on pastures with older goats

d how resting a pasture helps to control disease

3 Say how each of the following chemicals is used on a goat farm:

a iodine

b copper sulphate solution

c sulphur of lime

d sevin powder

e antibiotics

4 Say why

a fodder grasses for goats or sheep should be hung or placed on a rack.

b goats with overgrown hair coats should be clipped

c legumes should be planted in pastures

d goats' milk is recommended for babies and invalids

5 Say how the following differ from each other

a the rumen and the reticulum

b a maintenance ration and a production ration

c a fodder grass and a grazing grass

d whole milk and substitute milk

6 Give reasons why

a animals should be provided with mineral licks.

b colostrum should be fed to kids and lambs.

c the udder must be stripped of all its milk.

d goats should be dehorned.

e the Barbados Black Belly sheep is suitable for production in the Caribbean.

7 Say what a farmer should do if his goat is suffering from

a large roundworm of the stomach

b scours (diarrhoea)

c hoof rot

d mastitis

Appendix 1: Agricultural Chemicals

Fertilisers

Nitrogenous
Sulphate of ammonia
Nitrate of soda
Urea
Ammonium nitrate
Anhydrous ammonium gas

Phosphatic
Superphosphate
Bonemeal
Basic slag
Ammonium phosphate

Potassic
Muriate of potash
Sulphate of potash
Woodash

Plant protection

Insecticides
Diazinon
Fastac
Karate
Malathion
Primicid
Sevin

Fungicides
Copper fungicide, e.g. kocide 101
Sulphur fungicide – flowers of sulphur
Other fungicides – Dithane, Captan, Anvil, Polyram, Ridomil

Nematicides
Miral
Formaldehyde
Furadan
Marshal
Nemagon

Weedicides
Non-selective – Gramoxone, Reglone, Gramocil, Atila
Selective – Amiben, Excel, Fusilade, Gesaprim

Spreader-sticker
Agral
Spray-oils

Other useful chemicals

Iodine
Copper sulphate
Ferrous sulphate
Lime (calcium carbonate)
Dilute hydrochloric acid
Calcium hydroxide solution
Sodium hydroxide solution

Appendix 2

Some facts on insecticides

The chlorinated hydrocarbons

Examples: BHC, Aldrin, Dieldrin, Chlordane.
These compounds have low solubility in water and are very persistent in nature. They tend to accumulate in the fatty tissues of animals.

These chemicals have a slow toxic action on the nervous system. Their residual effects have proven to be very detrimental to the user and to those who have consumed crops sprayed with them. As a result, it is advisable that they should *not* be used in crop production programmes.

The organo-phosphorus compounds

Malathion is the most widely used chemical in this group. It controls insects such as weevils, beetles, thrips, aphids, mealy-bugs, leaf-hoppers and scale insects.

Malathion has a toxic action on the nervous system of the insect. It is quick-acting and has a short persistency. It is readily detoxified or broken down in the body tissues of animals. Other insecticides in this group are Dipterex, Rogor, and Meta-systox.

The carbamates

Sevin is the chief carbamate in use. It is a general purpose insecticide and controls a number of insects by acting upon their nervous systems. The chemical is safe to use, as it is readily broken down and eliminated from the body tissues of animals.

Safety precautions in the use of chemicals

Pesticides should be properly stored and kept out of the reach of children and animals.

Ensure that pesticide containers are labelled and kept free from leaks.

Use chemical dosages as recommended by the manufacturers.

Spray cans and dusting equipment must be kept clean and in good working order.

Stop spraying crops at least two weeks before harvesting the crops for sale or for consumption.

Empty pesticide containers must be burnt or buried.

Persons who use chemicals should protect themselves by using respirators, hand-gloves and proper clothing.

Index